THE KEY

STUDENT STUDY GUIDE

glish 20-1

THE KEY

THE KEY series of student study guides is specifically designed to assist students in preparing for unit tests, provincial achievement tests, and diploma examinations. Each **KEY** includes questions, answers, detailed solutions, and practice tests. The complete solutions show problem-solving methods, explain key concepts and highlight potential errors.

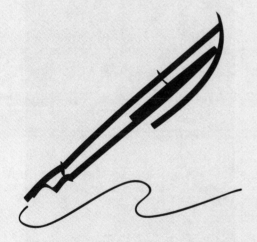

Reading

Listening

Viewing

Writing

Speaking

Representing

Canadian Cataloguing in Publication Data

Rao, Gautam, 1961 –
THE KEY – English 20-1 (AB)

1.   English – Juvenile Literature. I. Title

Published by
Castle Rock Research Corp.
2340 Manulife Place
10180 – 101 Street
Edmonton, AB T5J 3S4

5 6 7 FP 07 06 05

Printed in Canada

Publisher
Gautam Rao

Contributors
Richard Clayton
Rick Bookham
Bill Talbot

Dedicated to the memory of Dr. V. S. Rao

THE KEY – ENGLISH 20-1

THE KEY for English 20–1 has been developed to support classroom instruction and help students to prepare for quizzes, unit tests, and final exams. Working through practice questions that are modeled after the English 30 provincial exams will help to familiarize students with the test format and the types of questions that are typically used. An overview of the main sections of ***THE KEY*** follows.

I   ***KEY Factors Contributing to School Success*** provides students with examples of study and review strategies. Topics include information on learning styles, study schedules, and developing review notes.

II   ***Writing and Reading*** begins with an overview of, and strategies for, reading poetry, narratives and Shakespearian plays. The section provides suggestions for developing personal and critical/analytical responses using reference texts, and completing tests and in-class assignments.

III   ***KEY Strategies for Success on Exams*** explores topics such as common exam question formats and strategies for responding, directing words most commonly used, how to begin the exam, and managing test anxiety.

IV   ***Practice Examination*** includes a complete practice examination that has been created using a blueprint similar to the one used by Alberta Education for the English 30-1 provincial examination. Detailed solutions fully explain each answer.

THE KEY *Study Guides* are available for Biology 20, Chemistry 20, Physics 20, English 20-1, Mathematics 20 (Pure), and Social Studies 20. A complete list of ***THE KEY*** *Study Guides* available for grades 3 to 12 is included at the back of this book.

For information about any of our resources or services, please call Castle Rock Research Corp. at 780.448.9619 or visit our web site at http://www.castlerockresearch.com.

At Castle Rock Research, we strive to produce a resource that is error-free. If you should find an error, please contact us so that future editions can be corrected.

CONTENTS

KEY FACTORS CONTRIBUTING TO SCHOOL SUCCESS

WRITING

READING

KEY STRATEGIES FOR SUCCESS ON EXAMS

PRACTICE EXAMINATION

ANSWERS AND SOLUTIONS

APPENDICES

NOTES

KEY FACTORS CONTRIBUTING TO SCHOOL SUCCESS

NOTES

 # *KEY* FACTORS CONTRIBUTING TO SCHOOL SUCCESS

You want to do well in school. There are many factors that contribute to your success. While you may not have control over the number or types of assignments and tests that you need to complete, there are many factors that you can control to improve your academic success in any subject area. The following are examples of these factors.

- **REGULAR CLASS ATTENDANCE** – helps you to master the subject content, identify key concepts, take notes and receive important handouts, ask your teacher questions, clarify information, use school resources, and meet students with whom you can study

- **POSITIVE ATTITUDE AND PERSONAL DISCIPLINE** – helps you to come to classes on time, prepared to work and learn, complete all assignments to the best of your ability, and contribute to a positive learning environment

- **SELF-MOTIVATION AND PERSONAL DISCIPLINE** – helps you to set personal learning goals, take small steps continually moving toward achieving your goals, and to "stick it out when the going gets tough"

- **ACCESSING ASSISTANCE WHEN YOU NEED IT** – helps you to improve or clarify your understanding of the concept or new learning before moving on to the next phase

- **MANAGING YOUR TIME EFFICIENTLY** – helps you to reduce anxiety and focus your study and review efforts on the most important concepts

- **DEVELOPING 'TEST WISENESS'** – helps to increase your confidence in writing exams if you are familiar with the typical exam format, common errors to avoid, and know how the concepts in a subject area are usually tested

- **KNOWING YOUR PERSONAL LEARNING STYLE** – helps you to maximize your learning by using effective study techniques, developing meaningful study notes, and make the most efficient use of your study time

📖 KNOW YOUR LEARNING STYLE

You have a unique learning style. Knowing your learning style – how you learn best – can help you to maximize your time in class and during your exam preparation. There are seven common learning styles. Read the following descriptions to see which one most closely describes your learning preferences.

- **LINGUISTIC LEARNER** (sometimes referred to as an auditory learner) – learns best by saying, hearing and seeing words; is good at memorizing things such as dates, places, names and facts

- **LOGICAL/MATHEMATICAL LEARNER** – learns best by categorizing, classifying and working with abstract relationships; is good at mathematics, problem solving and reasoning

- **SPATIAL LEARNER** (sometimes referred to as a visual learner) – learns best by visualizing, seeing, working with pictures; is good at puzzles, imaging things, and reading maps and charts

- **MUSICAL LEARNER** – learns best by hearing, rhythm, melody, and music; is good at remembering tones, rhythms and melodies, picking up sounds

- **BODILY/KINESTHETIC LEARNER** – learns best by touching, moving, and processing knowledge through bodily sensations; is good at physic activities

- **INTERPERSONAL LEARNER** – learns best by sharing, comparing, relating, cooperating; is good at organizing, communicating, leading, and understanding others

- **INTRAPERSONAL LEARNER** – learns best by working alone, individualized projects, and self-paced instruction

(Adapted from http://snow.utoronto.ca/Learn2/mod3/mistyles.html)

Your learning style may not fit "cleanly" into one specific category but may be a combination of two or more styles. Knowing your personal learning style allows you to organize your study notes in a manner that provides you with the most meaning. For example, if you are a spatial or visual learner, you may find mind mapping and webbing are effective ways to organize subject concepts, information, and study notes. If you are a linguistic learner, you may need to write and then "say out loud" the steps in a process, the formula, or actions that lead up to a significant event. If you are a kinesthetic learner you may need to use your finger to trace over a diagram to remember it or to "tap out" the steps in solving a problem or "feel" yourself writing or typing the formula.

📖 SCHEDULING STUDY TIME

Effective time management skills are an essential component to your academic success. The more effectively you manage your time the more likely you are to achieve your goals such as completing all of your assignments on time or finishing all of the questions on a unit test or year-end exam. Developing a study schedule helps to ensure you have adequate time to review the subject content and prepare for the exam.

You should review your class notes regularly to ensure you have a clear understanding of the new material. Reviewing your lessons on a regular basis helps you to learn and remember the ideas and concepts. It also reduces the quantity of material that you must study prior to a unit test or year-end exam. If this practice is not part of your study habits, establishing a study schedule will help you to make the best use of your time. The following are brief descriptions of three types of study schedules.

- **LONG-TERM STUDY SCHEDULE** – begins early in the school year or semester and well in advance of an exam; is the **most effective** manner for improving your understanding and retention of the concepts, and increasing self-confidence; involves regular, nightly review of class notes, handouts and text material

- **SHORT-TERM STUDY SCHEDULE** – begins **five to seven days prior to an exam**; must organize the volume of material to be covered beginning with the most difficult concepts; each study session starts with a brief review of what was studied the day before

- **CRAMMING** – occurs the night before an exam; is the **least effective** form of studying or exam preparation; focuses on memorizing and reviewing critical information such as facts, dates, formulas; do not introduce new material; has the potential to increase exam anxiety by discovering something you do not know

Regardless of the type of study schedule you use, you may want to consider the following to maximize your study time and effort:

- establish a regular time and place for doing your studying

- minimize distractions and interruptions during your study time

- plan a ten minute break for every hour that you study

- organize the material so you begin with the most challenging content first

- divide the subject content into smaller manageable "chunks" to review

- develop a marking system for your study notes to identify key and secondary concepts, concepts that you are confident about, those that require additional attention or about which you have questions

- reward yourself for sticking to your schedule and/or completing each review section

- alternate the subjects and type of study activities to maintain your interest and motivation

- make a daily task list with the headings "must do", "should do", and "could do"

- begin each session by quickly reviewing what you studied the day before

- maintain your usual routine of eating, sleeping, and exercising to help you concentrate for extended periods of time

KEY STRATEGIES FOR REVIEWING

Reviewing textbook material, class notes, and handouts should be an ongoing activity and becomes more critical in preparing for exams. You may find some of the following strategies useful in completing your review during your scheduled study time.

READING OR SKIMMING FOR KEY INFORMATION

- Before reading the chapter, preview it by noting headings, charts and graphs, chapter questions.

- Turn each heading and sub-heading into a question before you start to read.

- Read the complete introduction to identify the key information that is addressed in the chapter.

- Read the first sentence of the next paragraph for the main idea.

- Skim the paragraph noting key words, phrases, and information.

- Read the last sentence of the paragraph.

- Repeat the process for each paragraph and section until you have skimmed the entire chapter.

- Read the complete conclusion to summarize each chapter's contents.

- Answer the questions you created.

- Answer the chapter questions.

CREATING STUDY NOTES

Mind Mapping or Webbing

- Use the key words, ideas or concepts from your reading or class notes to create a *mind map or web* (a diagram or visual representation of the information). A mind map or web is sometimes referred to as a knowledge map.

- Write the key word, concept, theory or formula in the centre of your page.

- Write and link related facts, ideas, events, and information to the central concept using lines.

- Use colored markers, underlining, or other symbols to emphasize things such as relationships, information of primary and secondary importance.

- The following example of a mind map or web illustrates how this technique can be used to develop an essay.

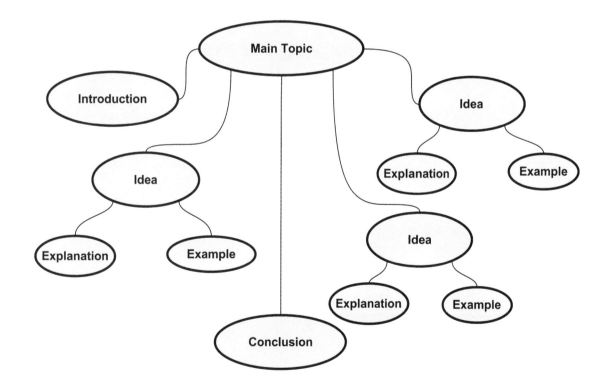

Copyright Protected

Charts

♦ Use charts to organize your information and relate theories, concepts, definitions, applications and other important details.

♦ Collect and enter the information in key categories.

♦ Use the completed chart as a composite picture of the concept or information.

The following is an example of how a chart can be used to help you organize information when exploring an issue in subjects such as Social Studies, the Sciences, or Humanities.

Define Key Words		
1.		
2.		
3.		
Explore the Issue		
Yes to the Issue	No to the Issue	Maybe to the Issue
1.	1.	1.
2.	2.	2.
3.	3.	3.
Case Studies and Examples		
1.	1.	
2.	2.	
3.	3.	
Defense of Your Point of View		
1.		
2.		
3.		

Index Cards

♦ Write a key event, fact, concept, theory, word or question on one side of the index card.

♦ On the reverse side, write the date, place, important actions and key individuals involved in the event, significance of the fact, salient features of the concept, essence and application of the theory, definition of the word or answer to the question.

♦ Use the cards to quickly review important information.

International System of Units (SI)

International System of Units (SI)

Base quantity	SI base unit	
	Name	Symbol
length	metre	m
mass	kilogram	kg
time	second	s
amount of substance	mole	mol

Derived Measures		
Measures	Unit	Symbol
Volume	cubic metre	m^3

SI Prefixes		
Factor	Name	Symbol
10^6	mega	M
10^3	kilo	k
10^{-2}	centi	c
10^{-3}	milli	m
10^{-6}	micro	μ

Symbols

♦ Develop your own symbols to use when reviewing your material to identify information you need in preparing for your exam. For example, an exclamation mark (!) may signify something that "must be learned well" because it is a key concept that is likely to appear on unit tests and the year-end exam. A question mark (?) may identify something you are unsure of while a star or asterisk (*) may identify important information for formulating an argument. A check mark (✓) or an (×) can be used to show that you agree or disagree with the statement, sentence or paragraph.

Crib Notes

- Develop brief notes that are a critical summary of the essential concepts, dates, events, theories, formulas, supporting facts, or steps in a process that are most likely to be on the exam.

- Use your crib notes as your "last minute" review before you go in to write your exam. You can not take crib notes into an exam.

MEMORIZING

- **ASSOCIATION** relates the new learning to something you already know. For example, in distinguishing between the spelling of 'dessert' and 'desert', you know 'sand' has only one 's' and so should desert.

- **MNEMONIC DEVICES** are sentences you create to remember a list or group of items. For example, the first letters of the words in the sentence "**E**very **G**ood **B**oy **D**eserves **F**udge" helps you to remember the names of the lines on the treble clef staff (E, G, B, D, and F) in music.

- **ACRONYMS** are words formed from the first letters of the words in a group. For example, **HOMES** helps you to remember the names of Canada's five Great Lakes (**H**uron, **O**ntario, **M**ichigan, **E**rie, and **S**uperior).

- **VISUALIZING** requires you to use your mind's eye to "see" the chart, list, map, diagram, or sentence as it exists in your textbook, notes, on the board, computer screen or in the display.

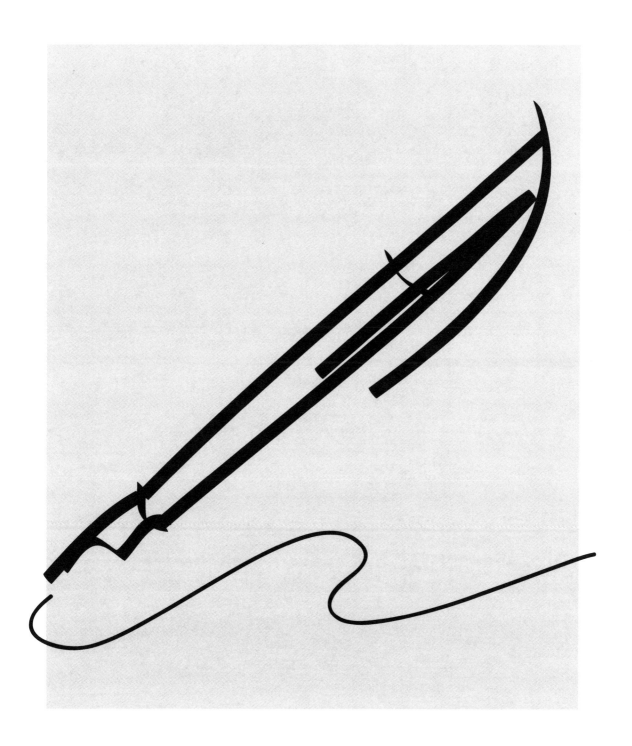

NOTES

INTRODUCTION

THE KEY for English 20–1 is a study guide that is designed to help you to meet the course outcomes that state that you are expected to listen, speak, read, write, view, and represent to:

- explore thoughts, ideas, feelings, and experiences
- comprehend literature and other texts in oral, print, visual, and multimedia forms, and respond personally, critically, and creatively
- manage ideas and information
- create oral, print, visual, and multimedia texts, and enhance the clarity and artistry of communication
- respect, support, and collaborate with others

☞ **The best way to meet these outcomes is to participate fully in all of your classroom learning activities, to read as many different literary works as possible by different authors, poets, and playwrights, and to practise effective reading, writing, and communication skills.**

☞ **Using this *KEY* will help you to practise your reading, writing, and communications skills, and give you strategies to supplement and reinforce your in-class work.**

GOAL SETTING

One of the keys to improving your English skills is to set personal goals for language growth. You may wish to use the following rubric that identifies some of the major English language arts skills in order to identify your strengths and areas for growth. Reviewing assignments and assessment rubrics from your current or past English language arts courses will help you to assess your strengths and areas that need improvement.

☞ **Use the strategies listed in this *KEY* and talk to your teacher about strategies for improvement.**

Skill	Yes	Needs Improvement
Read regularly		
Predict and ask questions while reading, discuss unfamiliar concepts with others		
Take note of words I am not sure of and use context or references to find meanings		
Go back to re-read passages to clarify meaning		
Use visualizing and graphic organizers as aids to analyzing text and planning for communicating ideas		
Connect what I am reading to what I know about and to other texts I have read		
Understand symbols, archetypes, and literary devices and use them to enhance understanding of texts		
Use ideas in texts to better understand and communicate understandings of self and the world around		

Skill	Yes	Needs Improvement
Know how to effectively introduce and conclude topics in writing or oral presentations		
Connect all ideas to a controlling idea		
Fully support ideas with explanations and examples		
Identify when ideas are not communicated clearly		
Use a variety of sentences and precise diction for effect		
Find and correct errors in spelling, usage, and punctuation		
Understand oral instructions		
Listen carefully, build on the ideas of others, ask questions to help others clarify ideas		
Comfortable making formal presentations		
Use voice effectively—volume, rate, tone, and pacing to communicate effectively and convey emotion		
Use eye contact and gestures for emphasis		
Use charts, graphs, visual aids to contribute to presentations		
Know how to find resources, effectively record information, and correctly reference sources		

☞ **Development of English language arts skills happens best when you have a personal purpose for engaging in reading writing, speaking, listening, viewing, and representing, and when these skill are integrated and support each other. For organizational purposes, the strategies in this *KEY* have been divided into reading and writing, but speaking, listening, viewing, and representing strategies have also been included.**

PERSONAL RESPONSE TO TEXT

Responding personally to the texts you have read helps you to bring more meaning to the texts and the contexts in which they were written. You can respond personally to texts and contexts in a variety of ways.

- If you personally connected with the experience of the character in a text, you could write a journal entry or poem to explore your ideas and feelings and therefore better understand your own experience.

- If you felt strongly about an issue raised by an idea, you could further investigate this issue, then create and show a multimedia presentation, or write a letter to a group such as Amnesty International to raise awareness or promote action.

- If you wanted to explore issues raised by a novel, you could create and present a dialogue where two characters debate their point of view of an event.

- If you found a statement by a character in a Shakespearean play interesting, disturbing, or provoking, you could write a rant and post on a personal blog in order to express your reaction.

Examples

Writing in response to the Beatrice's statement in *Much Ado about Nothing*, "I had rather hear my dog bark at a crow than a man swear he loves me," would allow you to express you ideas about relationships and romance. Writing in response to Polonius' statement in *Hamlet* that "the apparel oft proclaims the man," would allow you to make a statement about the importance (or lack of importance) of fashion.

⚷ **While much of your feedback on personal responses can come from an audience for whom you are writing, you can also use a rubric such as the one below to help you judge the effectiveness of your responses or parts of your responses.**

SCORING GUIDE FOR PERSONAL RESPONSE

Thought

5 An insightful understanding of the text is effectively demonstrated. Ideas are perceptive.

4 A well-considered understanding of the text is appropriately demonstrated. Ideas are thoughtful.

3 A defensible understanding of the text is clearly demonstrated. Ideas are straightforward.

2 An understanding of the text may be evident but is vaguely demonstrated or not always defensible or sustained. Ideas are over generalized and/or incomplete.

1 An implausible conjecture regarding the text is suggested. Ideas are incomprehensible or indefensible.

Support/Detail

5 Significant, precise, and deliberately chosen details enhance the ideas.

4 Relevant and purposeful details clarify the ideas.

3 Adequate but generalized details support the ideas.

2 Few details that are vaguely related to the ideas.

1 Irrelevant details or no details to support the ideas

Organization

5 Skilful organization provides coherence and direction. Effective beginnings and endings provide clear direction and proficiently conclude the ideas.

4 A controlled organization provides coherence and direction. Logical beginnings and endings introduce and conclude the ideas.

3 Organization is generally clear, but coherence may falter. Beginnings and endings are functional.

2 Faltering organization leaves the relationship between ideas unclear. Beginnings and/or endings are ineffective.

1 Non-functional organization leaves the purpose unclear. Beginnings and/or endings are vague and unfocused.

Language Use

5 Precise and effective use of diction and syntax with a confident voice that may be controlled for effect.

4 Carefully chosen diction and syntax with a specific and generally effective voice.

3 Clear but general diction with an appropriate voice.

2 Imprecise diction and awkward or unclear syntax with an uncontrolled or inappropriate voice.

1 Inaccurate diction and uncontrolled, confusing syntax with a lack of voice.

Correctness

5 Confident control of mechanics, punctuation, grammar, and word usage with a relative absence of errors, considering the complexity and length of the student's writing.

4 Competent control of mechanics, punctuation, grammar, and word usage with a relative absence of errors, considering the complexity and length of the student's writing.

3 General control of mechanics, punctuation, grammar, and word usage with occasional lapses in correctness that do not interfere with the meaning.

2 Limited control of mechanics, punctuation, grammar, and word usage with a range of errors that blur the clarity of meaning.

1 A lack of control of mechanics, punctuation, grammar, and word usage with a range of frequent and jarring errors that impede communication.

Scoring Guide for Personal Response: Adapted from Alberta Education, *English 20* (Teacher Manual: Classroom Assessment Materials, Project [CAMP]) (Edmonton, AB: Alberta Education, 1997), pp. 28–30, 33–35.

CRITICAL/ANALYTICAL RESPONSE TO TEXT

Writing critical/analytical responses can also lead you to a deeper understanding as you further investigate and analyze the texts and the contexts in which they were written.

Critical/analytical responses are written to a variety of different types of texts. In English 20-1, response to literary texts is emphasized and often takes the form of an essay. In a critical response, you are not limited to any one structure, but whatever you use, your writing should have a clear controlling idea that produces a unifying effect throughout the whole composition.

The **controlling idea** is basic to the essay. It is simply the familiar **topic**, or **theme,** or **thesis statement**. (In a paragraph, the controlling idea is called the topic. In literature, the controlling idea is called the theme. In an essay, it is called the thesis statement.) The controlling idea is what a piece of writing is about. Everything in a well-structured, well-organized work refers to the controlling idea.

In the context of a literary essay, **supporting detail** can refer to an actual detail, like a single incident, or a single scene description, or a single sensory image, or a single metaphor. At the same time, **supporting detail** can mean a discussion or explanation of plot or setting, or of the use of imagery or figurative language.

One way of writing a critical/analytical response to context is to examine the implications of what the text suggests.

Example

In the poem "two prisons divided by a gulf" by Jean Vanier (see page 35), the last line suggests that the gulf between a "miserable man" and a "man of means" needs to be bridged and asks who will do it. Analyzing what it means to be a bridge, and examining people or agencies who are currently trying to be that bridge, is one way of analyzing the context in which, and for which, the poem was created.

The second step in writing a response is to choose an appropriate form in which to respond. In this case, you could create a one or two page report on an organization or strategy designed to provide aid in the community or the wider world, to determine whether it is a legitimate way of helping others.

The first part of your report could include your findings about the organization and your conclusions about the validity of this way of helping people. Use questions to guide your research.

- What is the purpose of the program?
- Who benefits?
- What has it accomplished?
- How much money is used for the administration of the program or on advertising and where does this money come from?

The second section of your report could detail how you came to this conclusion, through an analysis and evaluation of your research, and the sources you used. This part of your report could be based on questions such as the following.

- Which information in your report was confirmed by more than one source?
- What are the primary and secondary sources you used to find information? What kind of information was in each? Which types were most relevant to your purpose and audience?
- Was the purpose of the information in each source to inform or persuade? How credible is this source? How do you know?
- Does the writer or organization providing the information have a vested interest? If so, what is it?

USING A MODEL

If you have difficulty in devising your own structure for essay writing, you may want to follow a straightforward structure such as the one modelled here that includes:

- an introductory paragraph that introduces your thesis and the text(s) that will be examined to support it
- three body paragraphs, each establishing and developing support for the thesis
- a concluding paragraph that unifies the writing

CREATE A THESIS STATEMENT

Your thesis statement often comes at the end of your introductory paragraph in order to provide guidance through the rest of your response. Your thesis statement contains the controlling idea for your essay. This idea may be either implicit in your thesis statement or may be stated explicitly.

☞ **Analysis of character, goal, conflict/obstacle, and realization/resolution should lead naturally to your thesis statement/controlling idea.**

Example

"Miss Brill," *a short story by Katherine Mansfield*

Character – Miss Brill is a woman who lives in a fantasy world. She imagines that she lives a glamorous life and that she plays an important part of the lives of others.

Goal – Contentment, escape from isolation of her real life

Conflict/obstacle – She is mocked by a young couple.

Realization/resolution – She eventually sees herself as others see her, realizes the loneliness and emptiness of her life, and is ultimately devastated.

Themes – Reality versus illusion, desire for companionship versus the struggle to belong

Thesis Statement (controlling idea is implicit) – Miss Brill lives in an imaginary world where she experiences a sense of contentment as she ———————— *Character/goal* imagines herself an important part of other people's lives. She is ———————— *Conflict* eventually forced to face the gloomy reality of the life she truly lives, and her feelings of contentment and self-worth are destroyed. ———————— *Realization/ resolution*

Controlling idea stated explicitly – Allowing imagination to blur one's reality can lead to both positive and negative consequences.

CREATE AN INTRODUCTORY PARAGRAPH

If you have difficulty with writing an introduction, here is a simple first paragraph template that you might find helpful.

- Write a sentence that introduces the topic and text(s) you will be using.
- Write several sentences that explain the topic and present your thesis statement, including the order of the evidence you will be supporting.

🔑 **Explore alternative beginnings to find the one that works best for the idea that you are developing. The first sentence is important because it introduces the mood and tone of your writing.**

Example

Introduces the topic "imagination" and the text selected

In the short story "Miss Brill," Katherine Mansfield depicts an elderly woman who lives within a fantasy world created by her imagination. She resorts to this world to escape from the isolation and loneliness of her real world and, by so doing, her life becomes more interesting and fulfilling. In her fantasy world, she experiences a sense of contentment as she imagines herself as an important part of other people's lives and as possessing a life better than those around her. Unfortunately, her fragile world is shattered, forcing her to face the gloomy reality of the life she truly lives. Her feelings of contentment and self-worth are destroyed once she realizes the emptiness and loneliness of her real world.

Thesis statement – opinion with the three supports identified as:

1. She experiences a sense of contentment

2. She imagines herself an important part of others lives

3. Her fragile world is shattered

CREATE YOUR DEVELOPING PARAGRAPHS

The first support for the main idea or the *thesis* is developed in Body Paragraph A, the second support for the thesis is developed in Body paragraph B, and the third support for the thesis is Body Paragraph C. Body Paragraphs B and C follow the same pattern as Body Paragraph A.

Each body paragraph contains the following elements:

- An effective introductory topic sentence that focuses on the aspect of support for the thesis that you will be developing in this paragraph.
- Development of your supporting idea by explaining it in a few sentences. To bring power to your position, you must include concrete *evidence* from the text(s). Direct quotations are only useful if they precisely support your idea. Direct references to events, character traits, literary symbols, etc. are all considered useful evidence.
- *Explain* your interpretation of the evidence in detail. Markers need to see evidence of your thinking. You need to demonstrate your intellect, your thinking, and your ability to interpret literature.
- *Elaborate* by specifically and overtly *connecting the information* in this paragraph to your thesis.
- A *transition sentence* must be considered. Transitions are necessary between paragraphs. They can happen at the end of paragraphs or in the introduction to a new paragraph.

Example Developing Paragraph A

Miss Brill is content and happy to live within her fantasy world; a world wonderful within her own mind. This world affords her delightful routines which, on most occasions, bring her to the Jardins Publiques where she enjoys the surroundings of nature, music, and people. On one particular Sunday afternoon, she dresses up for her outing, completing her ensemble with her fox fur piece; a piece she has had for a long time and of which she is very proud. From her position on a park bench, she watches and internally comments on what she sees. Miss Brill is a keen observer of the people around her and she weaves what she sees and hears into imaginative, glamorous events. She notices an elderly gentleman in a velvet coat, and a woman with knitting in her lap. She is disappointed that they are not speaking as she had become quite expert "at listening to people's conversations, as though she wasn't listening." She turns her attention to other people and their activities around her. As she sits, she does not ponder her own solitary life as she is happy to enjoy the splendour of the day.

Topic sentence clearly identifies the first support: she experiences a sense of contentment

Specific details from the story to demonstrate her contentment

Concluding sentence

Developing Paragraph B

Ironically, as Miss Brill observes the other people—especially those occupying benches and chair—she fails to see the parallel between herself and them. She notes that Sunday after Sunday, the same people are drawn to the park and something is "funny" about all of them. They were odd, silent, nearly all old, and from the way they stared, they looked as though they'd come from dark little rooms or even cupboards. She perceives these people as being different; as being "less" than what she is. As well, she does not see herself as being rejected like the violets the young woman throws away or like the woman in the ermine toque that is being carelessly cast aside by the man in the suit. Even more sad is that Miss Brill, wearing her own fur piece, cannot see her own image mirrored in the woman who appears to be as shabby as the ermine toque she wears. Miss Brill, rather, imagines herself as being superior to these people; an intricate part of the stage performance that is re-enacted in the park each week. She fantasizes that her absence would be noticed if she were not present, so integral is her role. She takes delight in this fantasy and envisions telling the old gentleman to whom she reads that she is not a mere English teacher, but an actress. She is enthralled by this fantasy and feels as though she is one with all the members of the company. Her imaginary world is, indeed, fulfilling.

Transition and topic sentence that clearly identifies the second support: imagining herself as superior to others, and an important part of their lives

Support, including symbols of her rejection that she ironically does not perceive

Concluding sentence

Developing Paragraph C

Transition and topic sentence that clearly identifies the third support: her fragile world is shattered

Support, including symbolism of her dark room and fur piece

Concluding sentence

Despite her excitement with her imaginary world, Miss Brill overhears a conversation which completely shatters her illusions and alters her life. A boy and girl, in love, sit near her, and Miss Brill prepares to listen. The boy wishes to kiss the girl but she insists that she cannot let him because of that stupid old thing at the end there. The girl then begins to giggle at the poor soul wearing the fur that looks like a fried whiting (fish). Miss Brill is shattered when she realizes that the young couple is mocking her. She leaves the park, not bothering to stop for her ritualistic slice of honey cake, and hurries home. Once inside, she realizes how dark her room is, like a cupboard. Her world is no longer bright and splendid, but depressing and stark in reality. This reality is even more bleak when compared to the imaginary world of her fantasies. Her fur piece symbolizes the shabbiness of her life, and as she replaces it in the box, she imagines she hears something crying. Although she seeks to deny that she is the one who is crying, she has come to an unhappy epiphany: the loneliness of her life is devastating.

CREATE A CONCLUDING PARAGRAPH

- Generalize your thesis beyond the text – make your idea explicit
- Summarize your major points
- End with a strong sense of closure

Example

Topic sentence explicitly states the controlling idea as a generalization beyond the text

Summary of support and significance of support

Thoughtful observation connected to resolution/effect on character

In "Miss Brill," Mansfield emphasizes both the positive and negative effects of the imagination, and what results when imagination is allowed to blur one's view of reality. Initially, Miss Brill is content living within the parameters of her fantasy world. Feelings of fulfillment are deepened as she perceives herself as being integral to the "performance" and the people around her; she views her own life as being "more" than what it truly is. When her illusion is shattered, however, the harshness of the reality she is compelled to face is devastating.

☞ **Learning to write a good critical/analytical response involves experimenting with different ways of responding until you find the way that works best for you.**

GROUP RESPONSE

Soliciting input from others while you are writing as well as asking for feedback on your final draft is an excellent way of improving your writing of critical/analytical responses. Working with one or two other people to write a group essay is one way of doing this. Work together to agree on a controlling idea, then divide the work up so that each person takes a different part to develop.

METHOD OF DEVELOPMENT

- One person writes the introduction discussing an issue raised in a poem and its relationship to the world.
- A second person writes the first developing paragraph discussing the poet's use of imagery and form to develop the controlling idea.
- A third person writes the second developing paragraph discussing how the poet's other choices develop the controlling idea.
- All participants work on a conclusion and agree on the best one to use.

☞ **Other methods of development such as organizing the developing paragraphs around similarities and differences or by the different stanzas in the poem are also valid as long as each contains all of the elements of an effective response (introduction, controlling idea, developing paragraphs, topic sentences, concluding sentences, supporting evidence and concluding paragraph).**

GROUP REVISION AND EDITING

Each person could be responsible for a different aspect of revision. For example, one could check to ensure that all ideas are explained and supported with specific details from the text; another could ensure that all details are connected to the controlling idea; and a third could work on effective transitions between ideas and paragraphs.

A similar cooperative approach can also be taken with editing of the work. For example, one person in the group could check for consistent verb tenses and pronoun references, another for spelling, and another for punctuation.

USING REFERENCE TEXTS

This is a good time to learn how to use reference texts effectively.

☞ **Do not leave learning this important skill until it is too late. You need to learn how to use a reference text before you write the diploma exam in Grade 12.**

1. A **dictionary** supplies word meanings, but has other uses that are sometimes overlooked. Look for these features in your dictionary, or look for them if you are choosing a dictionary.

   Words often have many meanings. The most useful dictionaries supply multiple meanings for words. This is helpful because the most common meaning may not fit the context of what you are reading. The more definitions the better.

Many dictionaries include usage notes that may contain:

- warnings about offensive words that are offensive in themselves or offensive in certain contexts
- warnings about easily confused words (like *insure*, *ensure*)
- usage notes on synonyms. These can help with precise diction. For example, an entry for *ridicule* might contain information like the following:

> *ridicule*—to make fun of with the intention of causing humiliation
>
> *deride*—to laugh scornfully
>
> *mock*—to make fun of by imitating appearance, actions, or words
>
> *taunt*—to call attention to someone's weaknesses

Words are broken into syllables and the syllable that receives the most stress is marked. This is very helpful when studying *metre*, or the rhythm of poetry.

The pronunciation guide can also be useful. When choosing a dictionary, look to see if the pronunciation guide is printed at the bottom of each page, and if a simple phonetic guide is used. As a pronunciation guide, a Canadian dictionary is best.

A good dictionary will list *idioms* or *idiomatic expressions* that are formed with an entry word. An idiom has a definite meaning, but it is not a literal meaning that could be figured out from the meaning of the individual words.

- *Monday week* means a week from next Monday.
- *Put upon* means taken advantage of.
- *Dropped off the radar* means forgotten, or overlooked.

2. **A thesaurus** can be very helpful if you are looking for the right word, but remember to read the instructions so that you know how the thesaurus is organized and how to choose words that fit the context and the audience.

☞ **It is easy to choose a word that is ridiculously wrong in a certain context. Be prepared to use a dictionary as well, or else use the thesaurus to remind you of words you already know.**

3. **Writing guides** contain a wealth of information on every step in writing and provide a handy reference for your questions about syntax, usage, grammar, and mechanics. Choose a guide that suits you and be prepared to spend the time to learn how to use it. One way to choose a writing guide is to make sure that it is designed to allow you to look up information easily and quickly.[*]

☞ **See Appendices C for a quick reference to syntax, grammar, and usage.**

---

[*] If you want to purchase a writing guide that is approved by Alberta Education for use on Part A of the Diploma Exam, consult the English 30 student guide found at http://www.education.gov.ab.ca/k%5F12/testing/diploma/guides/default.asp.

EVALUATE YOUR WRITING

Using a scoring rubric such as the following can help you to assess your writing strategies and areas that need improvement.

Scoring Guide for Critical Response to Literary Texts

Thought

5 Literary interpretations are perceptive and an insightful understanding and appreciation of the writer's choices are effectively demonstrated.

4 Literary interpretations are sensible and a thoughtful understanding of the writer's choices is demonstrated.

3 Literary interpretations are straightforward and defensible, and a clear understanding of the writer's choices is demonstrated.

2 Literary interpretations are incomplete and a limited understanding of the writer's choices is demonstrated.

1 Literary interpretations may not be defensible and little understanding of the writer's choices is evident.

Support/Detail

5 Well-defined, carefully chosen examples with precise explanations.

4 Well-defined, accurate examples with relevant explanations.

3 Appropriately chosen but conventional examples with general explanations.

2 Inappropriately chosen examples with underdeveloped explanations.

1 Irrelevant examples with misleading explanations or no explanations.

Organization

5 Purposeful organization provides coherence and direction. Effective beginnings and endings provide clear direction and skilfully conclude the ideas.

4 A controlled organization provides coherence and direction. Competent beginnings and endings introduce and conclude the ideas.

3 Organization is generally clear, but coherence may falter. Beginnings and endings are functional.

2 Faltering organization leaves the relationship between ideas unclear. Beginnings and/or endings are ineffective.

1 Non-functional organization leaves the purpose unclear. Beginnings and/or endings are vague and unfocused.

Matters of Choice

5 Confident and purposeful use of diction and syntax with a confident voice that may be controlled for effect.

4 Carefully chosen diction and syntax with an appropriate and generally effective voice.

3 Clear but general diction and syntax with an appropriate voice.

2 Imprecise diction and awkward or unclear syntax with an uncontrolled or inappropriate voice.

1 Inaccurate diction and uncontrolled, confusing syntax with a lack of voice.

Correctness

5 Confident control of mechanics, punctuation, grammar, and word usage with a relative absence of errors, considering the complexity and length of the student's writing.

4 Competent control of mechanics, punctuation, grammar, and word usage with a relative absence of errors, considering the complexity and length of the student's writing.

3 General control of mechanics, punctuation, grammar, and word usage with occasional lapses in correctness that do not interfere with the meaning.

2 Limited control of mechanics, punctuation, grammar, and word usage with a range of errors that blur the clarity of meaning.

1 A lack of control of mechanics, punctuation, grammar, and word usage with a range of frequent and jarring errors that impede communication.

Scoring Guide for Critical Response: Adapted from Alberta Education, *English 20* (Teacher Manual: Classroom Assessment Materials Project [CAMP]) (Edmonton, AB: Alberta Education, 1997), pp. 28–30, 33–35.

TESTS AND IN-CLASS ASSIGNMENTS

Tests and in-class assignments require you to work under specific time limits, which means that you often need additional strategies for quickly generating and organizing ideas, deciding on the controlling idea for your composition and choosing support. You can use different strategies, depending on the type of assignment or the wording of the question.

SPECIFIC TOPICS

In some assignments, your course of action is very clear and the controlling idea is implied.

Example

Writing assignment based on *Romeo and Juliet*: Romeo and Mercutio reveal their different personalities in their statements about love. Compare and contrast their personalities.

In this case, you know exactly what to do. If you know that Romeo has romantic and idealistic ideas about love, while Mercutio is cynical and bawdy, you have enough to write a **thesis statement**, or sentence that expresses the controlling idea. Even the pattern of organization is assigned: this is a **compare-and-contrast** essay.

OPEN-ENDED ASSIGNMENTS

Some questions are open-ended. There might be as many responses as there are students responding, and there is certainly not just one answer. Your controlling idea may only appear when you generate and organize your ideas about the topic.

Example

In literature, what is the effect of foretelling or prophecy?

1. Try brainstorming any ideas that you have about the topic, such as those in the following list:
    prophecy + foretelling
    Titanic 1912
    myth, play
    ancient Greece
    Sophocles' Oedipus play
    acting on foreknowledge = disaster
    Oedipus would kill father, marry mother
    Greece, child murder, exposure
    Oedipus = twisted
    father's death accidental
    another fulfillment if no murder?
    suicide, self-blinding
    accepting foretelling → total ruin
    no foretelling or prophecy
    Change history? yes vs. no
    Yes → action
    mystery, fate, partial understanding
    crime to avoid evil causes is cause of the evil

☞   **At this point, your idea may have emerged and you are ready to write. If not, you will have to do more organizing.**

2. Try combining brainstorming with creating a mind map. These are especially useful and flexible for connecting ideas in different ways.

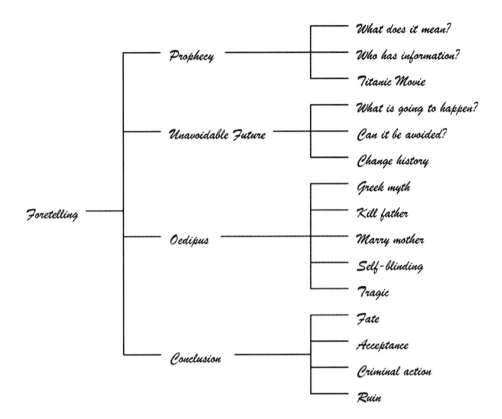

3. If your idea is still not clear, you may need to add more detail to each section, especially for longer, more complicated writing. Putting ideas into a prepared form can expose any gaps in your plan and any confusion in your organization. In this method of organizing, the headings and subheadings and the logical numbering system show the relative importance of each item.

I Introductory paragraph

    A. Topic sentence

        1. Motif

        2. Prophecy, foretelling

        3. Results

    B. Example

        Oedipus (Greek myth)—Avoidance leads to fulfillment

    C. Thesis statement

        1. Action based on foreknowledge a common theme

        2. Usually involves crime

        3. Always ends in disaster

II First body paragraph

    A. Prophecy when Oedipus born

        1. Kill father, king of Thebes

        2. Marry mother

        3. Horrified reaction

III Second body paragraph

    A. Action to avoid prophecy

        1. Decision to murder child

        2. Exposed on a hillside

            a. Death certain

            b. Murderer avoids knowledge of own actions

    B. Survival

        1. Rescue by shepherd

        2. Fostered by king of another city

IV Third body paragraph

    A. Fulfillment

        1. Kills father unwittingly in quarrel

        2. Marries a widow—his mother

        3. Both unaware

    B. Ruin

        1. Discovery

        2. Oedipus blinds self

V Concluding paragraph

    A. Foreknowledge partial

        1. Crimes lead to disaster

        2. Even good actions disastrous

        3. Actions are primary cause of disaster

B. Oedipus

    1. Without crime, might have become great king?

    2. "Marrying mother" might have meant benefiting his city (symbolically his "mother")?

C. Conclusion

    1. Partial knowledge dangerous

    2. Crimes committed to avoid evil directly cause the evil

    3. Even good intentions are dangerous

REVISING AND EDITING

On an in-class assignment or test, you have less time to revise and edit your work than in other assignments, so it is more important to observe your own thoughts and writing and judge how you are doing in order to guide your thoughts and actions as they unfold.

1. When outlining and writing, observe your writing and give yourself feedback. Ask yourself:

- Do all my ideas and observations fit the controlling idea?
- Do all the details fit the controlling idea?
- Is anything off-topic?
- If a good idea is off-topic, does that mean the controlling idea needs more thought?
- Is the controlling idea clearly expressed at the beginning of the essay?

☞   **If you are deliberately keeping the expression of the controlling idea for a point within the essay or at the end of it, then you must set up an organization to make this pattern work.**

2. The content itself must also be considered. Ask yourself:

- Are my responses to literature plausible? Are they supported by evidence from the literature, from other literature, or from other sources, such as personal observation or experience, or history, or science?
- Is my evidence accurate?
- Are quotations accurate?
- Are references accurate?
- Have I backed up my statements with explanations and evidence?

Example

The following is an example of a statement that is not backed up by evidence. Notice how the first sentence is just repeated with different words.

> *Hamlet is indecisive. He cannot make up his mind. He keeps changing his mind about things. Every time he is faced with a decision, he does not act.*

This statement backed up by evidence taken from the play.[†]

> *Hamlet is indecisive. He cannot decide whether the ghost is really his father or not. He puts off doing anything until he has found out the truth—and even then he does not act. He only moves against Claudius in the very last scene, when he realizes that Claudius has poisoned him.*

3. If the controlling idea and the content are sound, then it is time to consider the presentation. Ask yourself the following questions:

- Does the opening paragraph clearly and effectively introduce or set up the controlling idea?

- Does the development of the controlling idea proceed logically through the body paragraphs?

- Does the closing paragraph sum up the essay without simply repeating the first paragraph?

- Is each paragraph properly organized as a paragraph? Is there a logical development of ideas from the first sentence to the last?

PROOFREADING

1. There is a difference between a long-term assignment and the corrected first draft that is expected on a test. When there is plenty of time to check details and to write several drafts, then polished work is expected. When time is limited, a first draft with corrections is usually all that is required.

2. While most markers will consider errors in context where the number of errors is balanced against the length and complexity of the piece of writing, you will still be expected to demonstrate a basic level of knowledge and skill that is expected of English 20-1 students.

🔑 **Make sure to proofread carefully since any error that leads to confusion or misunderstanding will adversely affect your mark.**

MULTIPLE-CHOICE READING TESTS

At times, you may be writing multiple-choice reading tests in class. The reading part of your Grade 12 diploma exam is also in a multiple-choice format, so it is a good idea to learn basic strategies early. The following strategies give you some ways of approaching these kinds of tests.

STRATEGIES FOR ANSWERING MULTIPLE-CHOICE QUESTIONS

1. Do not look for patterns in the answer key.

2. Use your knowledge from the questions you have already answered to build your understanding for answering subsequent questions. Do not treat each question as a separate item.

3. If you do not know the answer, eliminate any unlikely responses, and then choose the best answer from those that are left.

4. If you are not sure of an answer, note on your exam booklet the questions that you want to reconsider, but do not change an answer unless you are sure that your first answer was wrong. Most of the time, your first impression is right.

5. If you find a question that is too difficult to answer, mark it and leave it for later.

[†] This is only an example; in fact, the play is too complex for such a simple argument.

6. Quickly scan the text you will be reading without pausing to study the details to determine:
   - the intended audience
   - what type of text it is (play, essay, report, short story, informal letter, formal letter, article, advertisement, …)
   - what the purpose of the writer is (to describe, to inform, to explain, to instruct, to persuade)
   - the general contents of the text

7. Note any information about the writer, or piece. If the writer's country of origin and/or dates of birth and death are given, it could provide you with very important information within the context of what was happening at that time in history to help you better understand the text.

8. Read the text using close reading strategies such as highlighting significant words in the questions or significant passages in the texts, or making notes in the margins as you read.

9. Connect the words on the page to what you already know. For example, if you like sports, reading the sports page is easy because you have developed a framework for reading, understanding, and storing information about sports.

10. Use reading strategies such as context and the structure of the word to figure out meaning, when the definitions are not given at the bottom of the page
    - Roots, prefixes, and endings can help you to find relationships between unfamiliar words and words that are familiar to you as a strategy for finding meaning.

Example 1

Consider the word "*aging*" in the phrase "*the population is aging rapidly.*" We recognize the word "*age*" in "*aging*" and therefore we can easily derive its meaning. Similarly the suffix "less" meaning "without" helps to understand the meaning of the word "ageless."
   - Using the context of a passage in which the word is used can help you to figure out meanings of unfamiliar words.

Example 2

The committee members left the boardroom close to midnight. Although they were exhausted after the sederunt, they agreed that we would meet again in the morning to complete the discussion.

You may not know the meaning of an unusual word like *sederunt*, but the context supplies the clues: committee, boardroom, midnight, exhausted, complete the discussion. You can quite confidently guess that a sederunt is a kind of meeting or discussion, probably a long one.

☞ **When you come across unfamiliar terms, check for footnotes first.**

11. If a question uses a quotation or a word from the text and gives line numbers, make sure to go back to the text to re-read those lines to better understand the quotation or word in the context in which it was used.

Example

The context of lines 43 to 67 suggests that the word disinterested *means*

>   **A.** *bored*
>   **B.** *unbiased*
>   **C.** *alienated*
>   **D.** *uninterested*

You may think that *uninterested* would be a safe choice. However, if these lines describe a fair-minded judge who listens with close attention to both sides of a case, then the context within the lines given would indicate the judge was *unbiased*.

> ☞ **Highlighting the lines in the text referred to in the question helps you to easily locate them.**

> ☞ **When a number of lines or a whole paragraph or verse are referred to in the question, make sure that you re-read all of the lines given. Reading only part of the lines will almost all ways lead you to the wrong answer.**

12. Use the features of the text to help you to determine meaning.

- The first paragraph of a non-fiction passage often contains the controlling idea or thesis statement. The main idea is also sometimes contained in the title and/or conclusion.
- Take particular note of titles and endings. Titles often give clues or reinforce meaning. Your interpretation of a text must take into account the ending. If you do not you often end up with an incomplete interpretation. An ending can sometimes entirely contradict an interpretation that ignores it.
- Characters' motives, goals, and attitudes central to understanding theme and are conveyed through the characters' description, actions, words, and thoughts.
- Use punctuation as important cues to meaning. Stopping at the end of a line of poetry when there is no punctuation for example, often breaks it up into meaningless chunks. In poetry, as in all writing, punctuation marks such as question marks and commas can clarify meaning; semicolons and colons can show relationships; and exclamation marks can help to reinforce mood.
- When reading scripts, use stage directions as important cues to meaning.

> ☞ **Use any pictures, graphs, and headings as important clues to determining meaning.**

> ☞ **Even though you may find some of the readings on the exam confusing or difficult, it is important to persevere. When the passage stops making sense, go back and reread, until it does make sense. You may need to read some poems several times to understand them.**

> ☞ **Use the practice exams at the end of this *KEY* to improve your skills in writing multiple-choice reading tests.**

READING

Introduction

Reading for English 20–1 requires critical and analytical reading skills and the development of close reading to understand contextual elements and subtext. The following strategies, using the poem "two prisons divided by a gulf" by Jean Vanier, are intended to help you to do this.

1. **Start with what you already know or can find out and connect it to the text.** In this case, you may want to start with the poet. If you research Jean Vanier, you can find out that he is a theologian and philosopher who strongly believes that community can change the world. He is also a person who acts on his beliefs, as he has devoted his life to the well-being of mentally and physically handicapped adults.

2. **You can now use this knowledge in your reading of the poem to help you to think about possible topics that Vanier might address as well as purposes and audiences for his writing.** As you read, you will also want to take note of the effects of the choices Vanier has made in his poem and how these contribute to meaning. This interplay between context and text will bring you to a deeper understanding of the poem.

the miserable man
i treat you as a stranger…
you were born and reared in
squalor…
you are walled in, for you have
no life
in front of you…no joys to
look
forward to…no loving
children
no esteem

t w o   p r i s o n s

d i v i d e d

with my clean clothes, my
sensitive nose (i hate bad
smells)
my politeness…a warm
house

b y

a world of security…the light
of reality does not penetrate my
cell, the reality of human

a

misery
so widespread, so deep…

g u l f

two prisons divided by a gulf: the miserable
man….
and imprisoned in the cell next door, the man
of means
comfortably installed…and so the world
goes on,
and the gulf gets wider

who will be the bridge

3. **Determine the speaker, to whom he is speaking, his subject, and his attitude toward that subject.** In this poem, the speaker refers to himself as a "man of means" and contrasts himself to the "miserable man" who was "born and reared in squalor." If you are not sure of the meanings of any of the words in the poem, be sure to look them up, since every word in a poem is chosen for its impact. In this case "means" refers to income or wealth, while "reared in squalor" refers to being brought up in filth or wretchedness (misery).

   You should then bring your background knowledge to bear, to think about any people that you are aware of that live in wealth, and those who live in miserable living conditions.

4. **Examine the poet's other choices in order to reinforce, revise, and extend the meaning that you have determined so far.** Imagery is always important. Vanier uses prison imagery in the title and the speaker refers to his own world as a cell which the light of reality does not penetrate, and refers to the miserable man as being walled in. This prison imagery suggests that both men are trapped, one by his poverty and the other by his complacency. Here, the light imagery, representing knowledge or understanding, is used to show how the speaker is unable or unwilling to understand the reality of the miserable man's world. Finally, in the last stanza, bridges are used to suggest that a connection between the two worlds is necessary and perhaps possible.

   This imagery is reinforced by the structure of the poem, where the title separating the worlds into two separate cells reinforces the gulf between the two. The fact that the two worlds are bridged by the last stanza reinforces the idea that the two can connect, that the gap between them can be bridged in order to build a world community.

5. **Now that you have extended your interpretation of the poem, examine any other choices that you have noted to reinforce your interpretation.** If you examine Vanier's use of alliteration, you will find that he uses the same alliteration (repetition of the letter "m") when describing the two men, reinforcing the idea that they are both the same—imprisoned in their worlds.

   Considering Vanier's choice of punctuation can also contribute to your interpretation. The use of a small "i" when the speaker refers to himself suggests a lack of importance and could reinforce the idea of equality; i.e., the man of means is no more important nor does he have more value than the miserable man. The use of ellipses suggests that the problem is on-going. There is no resolution yet, but something is coming next. Finally, the lack of a question mark after the question "who will be the bridge" could imply that it is not really a question at all, but a statement—perhaps a call to action to the man of means who is the only one of the two with the resources to be the bridge.

POETRY

In "two prisons divided by a gulf," as in any poem, various elements work together to create meaning. It is therefore important to understand the various elements of poetry so that you can use them to help you in your analytical and critical reading of poems.

1. Know the poetic devices, such as images and symbols, that are used to add or enhance meaning.

   - A **metaphor** is a comparison made by referring to one thing as another.
      Example: His anger was a storm forming in the horizon.
   - **Personification** is the attribution of human characteristics to non-human things.
      Example: Shakespeare's "Blow, blow, thou winter wind, / Thou art not so unkind / As man's ingratitude; / Thy tooth is not so keen" contains both an apostrophe and personification. (Apostrophe: the poem is addressed to the winter wind. Personification: the wind is said to be unkind and to have a tooth; both are human attributes).
   - A **simile** is a comparison using the word *like* or the word *as*.
      Example: …an eager spirit like a bright flame.
   - **Allusion** is a reference to a pre-existing work of art or literature, or to a person or event.
   - **Symbols** are objects used to represent ideas.
      Example: Sunrises represent new beginnings.
   - **Synecdoche** is a figure of speech in which a part of something is used to stand for the whole thing.
      Example: Many hands make light work. (Hands refer to people).
   - **Metonymy** is a figure of speech in which an attribute of a thing or something associated with the thing stands for the thing itself.
      Example: The suits make the decisions around here. (Suits refer to managers).
   - An **apostrophe**[*] is a statement, question, or request addressed to someone who is dead or absent, or to an inanimate objects.

   👉 **Make sure that you know common symbols and archetypes. See Appendix A at the back of this book for a list.**

2. Know the devices that are used to evoke images and sound. Reading a poem with attention to these will help you to understand the mood, atmosphere, feelings, and emotion that the poet wants to convey. For example, repetition of soft sounds such as "s" or "m" can reinforce a peaceful mood, while repetition of harsh sounds can reinforce the idea of conflict.

   - **Alliteration** is the repetition of initial consonants.
      Example: Lo, praise of the prowess of people-kings[†].
   - **Assonance** is the repetition of vowel sounds in stressed syllables.
      Example: I had to laugh to see the calf walk down the path a mile and half.
   - **Consonance** is the repetition of consonant sounds.
   - *Example:* The lady lounged lazily by the pool.
   - **Dissonance** is the use of discordant or unpleasant sounds.
   - **Half rhyme** is consonance on final consonants; it is usually proceeded by different final vowel sounds.
   - *Example:* From the ground, he picked the staff, And looking back, he hurried off.
   - **Onomatopoeia** is the use of words that suggest the sound of the thing they describe.
   - *Example:* Tennyson's "murmuring of innumerable bees" imitates the sound of bees.

---

[*] Do not confuse this apostrophe with the punctuation mark (')

[†] From Beowulf

- **Rhyme** is the repetition of same sounds. Syllables, entire words, or groups of words can rhyme. As a rule, rhyme consists of the last stressed vowel and all the sounds after it. (infernal/eternal; laughter/rafter; ring high/sing high). Rhyme is usually found at the end of a line of poetry, but sometimes it occurs within the line (internal rhyme).

- **Rhythm and Verse** Poets work with these variable rhythms of speech through the deliberate intensification and patterning of rhythm and also through the deliberate intensification of the images and emotions that are invoked by words. The three most common types of verse in English poetry are:

   a) Metrical verse, which is written with a strongly patterned rhythm. The metre guides the reading of metrical verse, and some of the meaning is carried by the rhythm. It is also called conventional verse.

   b) Free verse, which does not have regular metrical or rhyme patterns. It often has definite, though variable, rhythms that resemble the cadence of everyday speech. Free verse may be rhymed or unrhymed, but any rhymes that do occur are likely to be irregular and may not occur at the end of lines.

   c) Blank verse, which is unrhymed poetry that is written in iambic pentameters.

NARRATIVE

Reading narratives involves many of the same close reading skills and knowledge of many of the same elements as does reading poetry, but there are some elements that are distinctive to each form of writing. The elements of narratives work together to create meaning, just as the elements of poetry do. Whether you are reading/viewing stories, novels, plays or films, a good understanding of these elements will help you to improve your analytical and critical reading of narratives.

PLOT

The sequence of events in a story makes up the **plot**. This is often described with the familiar plot diagram shown below, although there are other possible structures.

A Plot Diagram

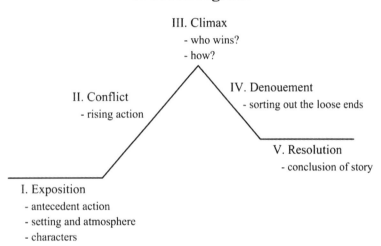

Part I establishes the main characters, the situation, and the problem (or conflict).

Parts II and III show the main characters' responses—the way they act and react, how they deal with the situation, the issues, the complications, the conflict, and the struggles.

Parts IV and V show how the characters are affected by events and show the results of their actions.

CHARACTER

The study of character involves examining character traits—qualities like courage, honesty, generosity, and intelligence—and their opposites, as well as the fundamental ideas and beliefs held by the character. These are revealed through direct and indirect characterization.

Direct characterization is *received*	Indirect characterization is *inferred*
• from what other characters say or think about the character	• from what the character says—sometimes from what the character says about another character
• from the writer's statements about the character. For example, "Jane was stubborn and persevering."	• from what the character thinks about self, others, and the world
	• from what the character does, especially in small things or when under pressure
	• from other characters reactions to the character

CONFLICT

Conflict is the problem that drives the action of a story. The conflict in a story may involve struggle and enmity, but that need not be the case. When Sherlock Holmes is solving a mystery, there is often no conflict in the sense of disagreement between the characters. The mystery itself is the conflict in the story.

There may be many problems in a complex story, but when speaking of conflict as one of the elements of narrative, it usually means the main problem that drives the story as a whole. On the other hand, a detailed analysis of a novel may have to take into account the conflict in each chapter and even the conflict in each scene.

Conflict may be analyzed in several ways. One way is to classify problems as *internal* or *external*.

Internal	External
• Characters struggle within themselves. They struggle with conscience, emotions, destructive character traits, or with conflicting desires or principles. • Internal conflict can be complicated and also combined with external conflict. An inner conflict over values, for example, can be part of a conflict with society's values.	• Characters may struggle with other characters because of hatred, disagreement, or misunderstanding. There may be a struggle between good and evil. There may be conflicting ideas about what is good—a clash of ideals. It is even possible for all the characters to be working together while problems arise from "the conflict." • Characters may struggle with entire groups of people—the problem may be with society. • Characters may struggle with universal problems like war, disease, poverty, or alienation. • Characters may struggle with nature in the form of wild weather, hostile terrain, or savage animals. • Characters may struggle with the unknown, with mysteries of any kind: with ghosts, miracles, alien abductions, the final mystery of death—or with the theft of a diamond necklace.

SETTING AND ATMOSPHERE

Setting is time and place. It serves at least one of three purposes:

1. to enrich the story with a physical world that contains real weather, plants, animals, countryside, cities, smells, sounds, and textures

2. to provide a real world of people, beliefs, ideas, and events—the kind of world that real people live in

3. to supply, or to contribute to, the atmosphere. Think of the dark and stormy night on which the young heroine arrives at the gloomy castle. On the other hand, sometimes the setting can be a contrast to the atmosphere. Think of bad news being received on Christmas Day.

Atmosphere is the mood, the overall feeling that a story produces. It is the atmosphere that produces emotional reactions in the reader: amusement, pity, horror. Imagery is often used to build atmosphere.

POINT OF VIEW

How the story is told affects your interpretation of the events and understanding of the story and is therefore important to consider. The chart below demonstrates how use of different points of view can affect the reader's knowledge of events and other characters.

Point of View	How the Story is Told	Narrators
First Person	The story is told by one of the characters in the story ("I"). The narrator is in the story.	**First person narrators** only know what they, themselves, think, feel, do, and see.
Third Person	The story is told through the eyes of one or more characters ("he, she, they"). The narrator is outside of the story, and tells what the characters think, feel, and do.	**Omniscient narrators** know about everything that happens and what any character thinks and feels. They can enter the mind of any character.
		Limited omniscient narrators only know about one character and the things that that one character knows, thinks, feels, and does. They can enter the mind of only one character.
Objective or Dramatic	The story is told without telling any characters' thoughts and feelings. Only the characters' actions and words are told. This point of view is a lot like the camera's point of view in a movie.	The **objective** or **dramatic narrator** knows only what a camera can record. Thus this storytelling form suffers from the limitations of film—but at the same time can produce a film-like effect.

THEME

The theme is the controlling idea that determines everything from the choice of characters to the choice of words and the events of the plot. A large work, like a novel, may have secondary themes, and theme can be discussed at more than one level—disagreement or at least varying approaches are common when theme is analyzed.

Example

The poet Tennyson, after the sudden death of a friend who was engaged to his sister, wrote *In Memoriam*, a series of poems. The theme of the poems is *death*. Yet the theme is also *mourning*. The theme could also be said to be *hope*, since Tennyson looked beyond death and grief to life after death. Each of these themes could be successfully defended.

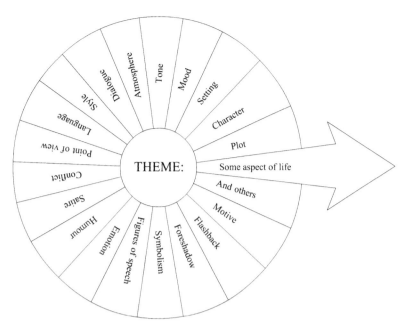

Since all elements of a narrative contribute to theme, an analysis of the various elements can lead us to an understanding of the themes of a text. The following is one way of analyzing a narrative.

- Start by examining a character's qualities and goals. What is the character like? What does he want? What is his goal?
- Determine the conflicts or obstacles the character faces in pursuit of these goals. What is the character's response to these obstacles? How does he feel? What does he do? Consider whether the setting and atmosphere have affected the character's responses and how the point of view affects your understanding of the character and his responses.
- Examine the resolution. What does the character learn or how does he change as a result of these experiences? What impact do these changes or realizations have on the character?
- Use your analysis of the character's response to the conflicts, the resulting changes and realizations and the impact of these on the character to determine themes that the text deals with and what the text says to you regarding these themes.

Example

"Touching Bottom," a short story by Kari Strut

Character – The protagonist is a young girl who seems to be quite fearful and insecure.

Goal – Security; her early experiences lead to the perception that she must rely on others for security and guidance. She relies on her father to provide security and guidance but as she grows older, she transfers this by marrying an older man.

Conflict/Obstacles – Moving to a new country, and her husband's infidelity, both isolate her and force her to rely on herself. This new setting contributes to her isolation that leads to her change in behaviour.

Resolution/Realization – When she needs to save herself and her stepson from drowning, she has no one but herself to rely on, and she consequently overcomes her fears and finds the strength and resourcefulness to survive. Realizing that she does not have to be reliant on others, she leaves her husband and creates a new life for herself. The impact of her realization is empowerment.

Theme – The themes of the story deal with perception, self-reliance, resourcefulness, and empowerment. The story might suggest to you that our perceptions of ourselves can limit us, but once we are forced to rely on ourselves we can recognize our own inner strength and overcome these limitations.

⚷ **Use other elements of literature, such as symbolism, to reinforce your understanding of character, plot, and theme. For example, in "Touching Bottom," water is used to represent danger at the beginning of the story to reinforce the character's feelings and to represent rebirth at the end to reinforce the change in character.**

SHAKESPEAREAN PLAYS

Reading Shakespeare poses a different challenge from most of your reading in English 20–1 because of the unfamiliar language. It is not nearly as difficult as it may appear; however, if you prepare properly for reading, build your understanding of Shakespearean English, and use specific reading strategies.

1. Read up on the background to the play so that you are not reading it cold. Understand who the characters are, where the play is set, and the basic plot.

🔑 **This step is essential, even for many people who are quite experienced in reading Shakespeare.**

2. If there are a number of characters in the play, draw a quick character map that shows how they are related to each other. Go back to this map whenever you get confused about who a character is.

3. Read the introduction to each scene, as this often contains a summary. Go back to read this information if you get confused about what is going on.

4. Know some basic Shakespearean expressions like the following:
    Pronouns

    Thou – *you* (subject); "Thou art a villain"
    Thee – *you* (object); "I shall give it to thee"
    Ye – *you* (plural); "Ye shall all be slain"
    Thy – *your*; "Here is thy sheath"
    Thine – *your* (before a vowel); "Thine eyes are like stars"
        or *yours*; "This dagger is thine"

    Verb conjugations

Infinitive	I	Thou	He/she/it
To have	have	hast	hath
To be	am or be	art	is or be
To do	do	dost	doth
To go	go	goest	goeth

    Contractions
        E'en – *even* or *evening*
        Tis, twas, t'were – *it is, it was, it were*
        Th' – *the*
        O' – *on* or *of*
        O'er – *over*
        Ne'er – *never*
        On't – *on it*
        Is't – *is it*

5. Use what you know of Shakespeare's unusual use of words.

Examples

- "a" was sometimes used to mean "he"
- A letter was sometimes dropped in order to silence an unwanted syllable: 'gainst, o'er, overpass'd.
- An extra syllable is sometimes added by pronouncing a silent syllable. (These are often accented: agèd, wearièd).
- The word "his" was sometimes used after a noun to indicate the possessive, as in, "Once, in a sea-fight 'gainst the Count his galleys"[*] (Once, in a sea-fight against the Count's ships).
- The masculine pronouns "him" and "his" were sometimes used for the neuter, "its" as in "How far that little candle throws his beams!"[†]
- One part of speech was frequently used to do the work of another part of speech. Nouns were used as adjectives, adjectives as verbs, and so on, as in the following lines where the word *candy*, normally a noun or verb, is used as an adjective.
- Why, what a candy deal of courtesy
- This fawning greyhound then did proffer me![‡]
- Words were sometimes omitted as in "…he shall with speed to England"[§]

6. Read to get a sense of what is happening—not to understand every word. Paraphrase what you understand if necessary.

Example

From *Much Ado about Nothing*, Act 1, Scene 1

Leonato: How many gentlemen have you lost in this action?
(How many have been killed in this battle?)

Messenger: But few of any sort and none of any name.
(Not many and no one important.)

Leonato: A victory is twice itself when the achiever brings home full numbers. I find here that Don Pedro hath bestowed much honour on a Young Florentine called Claudio.
(Winning is sweeter when you don't lose many soldiers. I see Don Pedro has honoured Claudio, a young man from Florence.)

Messenger: Much deserved on his part and equally remembered by Don Pedro. He hath borne himself beyond the promise of his age, doing in the figure of a lamb, the feats of a lion. He hath indeed better bettered expectation than you must expect of me to tell you how.
(It was well deserved since he fought better than you would expect from someone so young.)

7. Carefully read footnotes and side notes.

---

[*] From *Twelfth Night*
[†] From *The Merchant of Venice*
[‡] From *Henry IV, Part I*
[§] From *Hamlet*

8. Look for phrases or words that restate other phrases or words.

    Example:

    > *Will all great Neptune's ocean wash this blood*
    > *Clean from my hand? No; this my hand will rather*
    > *The multitudinous seas incarnadine,*
    > *Making the green one red.*[*]

    The last phrase restates *incarnadine* in more familiar words, "making the green red." Therefore, to *incarnadine* something is to make it red; in this case, to make the green seas red. (*Even the ocean can not wash my hands clean. My hands will turn the ocean blood red*).

9. If the syntax of a line is confusing, change the word order to a more understandable order.
    - Example:

    The line from *The Tragedy of King Richard The Second,* "When my poor heart no measure keeps in grief" could be restated as, "when my poor heart keeps no measure in grief".

⌐→   **Viewing the play or a film version of the play can make Shakespeare easier to understand because you derive meaning from the character's gestures and facial expressions in addition to the words. Remember that you must also be able to understand the written text.**

---

[*] From King Henry VI, Part I

KEY STRATEGIES

FOR

SUCCESS ON EXAMS

NOTES

 # *KEY* STRATEGIES FOR SUCCESS ON EXAMS

There are many different ways to assess your knowledge and understanding of course concepts. Depending on the subject, your knowledge and skills are most often assessed through a combination of methods which may include performances, demonstrations, projects, products, and oral and written tests. Written exams are one of the most common methods currently used in schools. Just as there are some study strategies that help you to improve your academic performance, there are also some test writing strategies that may help you to do better on unit test and year-end exams. To do your best on any test, you need to be well prepared. You must know the course content and be as familiar as possible with the manner in which it is usually tested. Applying test writing strategies may help you to become more successful on exams, improve your grades, and achieve your potential.

📖 STUDY OPTIONS FOR EXAM PREPARATION

Studying and preparing for exams requires a strong sense of self-discipline. Sometimes having a study buddy or joining a study group

- helps you to stick to your study schedule
- ensures you have others with whom you can practice making and answering sample questions
- clarifies information and provides peer support

It may be helpful to use a combination of individual study, working with a study buddy, or joining a study group to prepare for your unit test or year-end exam. Be sure that the study buddy or group you choose to work with is positive, knowledgeable, motivated, and supportive. Working with a study buddy or a study group usually means you have to begin your exam preparation earlier than you would if you are studying independently.

Tutorial classes are often helpful in preparing for exams. You can ask a knowledgeable student to tutor you or you can hire a private tutor. Sometimes school jurisdictions or individual schools may offer tutorials and study sessions to assist students in preparing for exams. Tutorial services are also offered by companies that specialize in preparing students for exams. Information regarding tutorial services is usually available from school counsellors, local telephone directories, and on-line search engines.

📖 EXAM QUESTION FORMATS

There is no substitute for knowing the course content. To do well in your course you need to combine your subject knowledge and understanding with effective test writing skills. Being familiar with question formats may help you in preparing for quizzes, unit tests or year-end exams. The most typical question formats include multiple choice, numerical response, written response, and essay. The following provides a brief description of each format and suggestions for how you might consider responding to each of the formats.

MULTIPLE CHOICE

A multiple choice question provides some information for you to consider and then requires you to select a response from four choices, often referred to as distracters. The distracters may complete a statement, be a logical extension or application of the information. In preparing for multiple choice questions you may wish to focus on:

- studying concepts, theories, groups of facts or ideas that are similar in meaning; **compare and contrast their similarities and differences**; ask yourself "How do the concepts differ?", "Why is the difference important?", "What does each fact or concept mean or include?" "What are the exceptions?"

- **identifying main ideas, key information**, formulas, concepts, and theories, where they apply and what the **exceptions** are

- memorizing important definitions, examples, and applications of key concepts

- learning to **recognize** *distracters* that may lead you to apply plausible but incorrect solutions, and *three and one splits* where one answer is obviously incorrect and the others are very similar in meaning or wording

- **using active reading techniques** such as underlining, highlighting, numbering, and circling important facts, dates, basic points

- making up your own multiple choice questions for practice

NUMERICAL RESPONSE

A numerical response question provides information and requires you to use a calculation to arrive at the response. In preparing for numerical response questions you may wish to focus on:

- memorizing formulas and their applications
- completing chapter questions or making up your own for practice
- making a habit of **estimating the answer** prior to completing the calculation
- paying special **attention to accuracy** in computing and the use of significant digits where applicable

WRITTEN RESPONSE

A written response question requires you to respond to a question or directive such as "explain", "compare", contrast". In preparing for written response questions you may wish to focus on:

- ensuring your response **answers the question**
- recognizing **directing words** such as "list", "explain", "define"
- providing **concise answers** within the time limit you are devoting to the written response section of the exam
- identifying subject content that lends itself to short answer questions

ESSAY

An essay is a lengthier written response requiring you to identify your position on an issue and provide logical thinking or evidence that supports the basis of your argument. In preparing for an essay you may wish to focus on:

- examining **issues** that are relevant or related to the subject area or **application of the concept**
- comparing and contrasting two points of view, articles, or theories
- considering the merits of the opposite point of view
- identifying **key concepts**, principles or ideas
- providing **evidence**, examples, and **supporting information** for your viewpoint
- preparing two or three essays on probable topics
- **writing an outline** and essay within the defined period of time you will have for the exam
- understanding the "marker's expectations"

📖 *KEY* TIPS FOR ANSWERING COMMON EXAM QUESTION FORMATS

Most exams use a variety of question formats to test your understanding. You must provide responses to questions ranging from lower level, information recall types to higher level, critical thinking types. The following information provides you with some suggestions on how to prepare for answering multiple choice, written response and essay questions.

MULTIPLE CHOICE

Multiple choice questions often require you to make fine distinctions between correct and nearly correct answers so it is imperative that you:

- begin by answering only the questions for which you are certain of the correct answer

- read the question stem and formulate your own response before you read the choices available

- read the directions carefully paying close attention to words such as "mark *all* correct", "choose the *most* correct" and "choose the *one best* answer"

- use active reading techniques such as underlining, circling, or highlighting critical words and phrases

- watch for superlatives such as "all", "every", "none", "always" which indicate that the correct response must be an undisputed fact

- watch for negatives such as "none", "never", "neither", "not" which indicate that the correct response must be an undisputed fact

- examine all of the alternatives in questions which include "all of the above" or "none of the above" as responses to ensure that "all" or "none" of the statements apply *totally*

- be aware of distracters that may lead you to apply plausible but incorrect solutions, and 'three and one splits' where one answer is obviously incorrect and the others are very similar in meaning or wording

- use information from other questions to help you

- eliminate the responses you know are wrong and then assess the remaining alternatives and choose the best one

- guess if you are not certain

WRITTEN RESPONSE

Written response questions usually require a very specific answer. In answering these questions you should:

- underline key words or phrases that indicate what is required in your answer such as "<u>three reasons</u>", "<u>list</u>", or "<u>give an example</u>"
- write down rough, point-form notes regarding the information you want to include in your answer
- be brief and only answer what is asked
- reread your response to ensure you have answered the question
- use the appropriate subject vocabulary and terminology in your response
- use point form to complete as many questions as possible if you are running out of time

ESSAY

Essay questions often give you the opportunity to demonstrate the breadth and depth of your learning regarding a given topic. In responding to these questions it may be helpful to:

- read the question carefully and underline key words and phrases
- make a brief outline to organize the flow of the information and ideas you want to include in your response
- ensure you have an introduction, body, and conclusion
- begin with a clear statement of your view, position, or interpretation of the question
- address only one main point or key idea in each paragraph and include relevant supporting information and examples
- assume the reader has no prior knowledge of your topic
- conclude with a strong summary statement
- use appropriate subject vocabulary and terminology when and where it is applicable
- review your essay for clarity of thought, logic, grammar, punctuation, and spelling
- write as legibly as you can
- double space your work in case you need to edit it when you proof read your essay
- complete the essay in point form if you run short of time

📖 *KEY* Tips for Responding to Common 'Directing' Words

There are some commonly used words in exam questions that require you to respond in a predetermined or expected manner. The following provides you with a brief summary of how you may wish to plan your response to exam questions that contain these words.

- ◆ **EVALUATE** (to assess the worth of something)
  - ▸ Determine the use, goal, or ideal from which you can judge something's worth
  - ▸ Make a value judgment or judgments on something
  - ▸ Make a list of reasons for the judgment
  - ▸ Develop examples, evidence, contrasts, and details to support your judgments and clarify your reasoning

- ◆ **DISCUSS** (usually to give pros and cons regarding an assertion, quotation, or policy)
  - ▸ Make a list of bases for comparing and contrasting
  - ▸ Develop details and examples to support or clarify each pro and con
  - ▸ On the basis of your lists, conclude your response by stating the extent to which you agree or disagree with what is asserted

- ◆ **COMPARE AND CONTRAST** (to give similarities and differences of two or more objects, beliefs, or positions)
  - ▸ Make a list of bases for comparing and contrasting
  - ▸ For each basis, judge similarities and differences
  - ▸ Supply details, evidence, and examples that support and clarify your judgment
  - ▸ Assess the overall similarity or difference
  - ▸ Determine the significance of similarity or difference in connection with the purpose of the comparison

- ◆ **ANALYZE** (to break into parts)
  - ▸ Break the topic, process, procedure, or object of the essay into its major parts
  - ▸ Connect and write about the parts according to the direction of the question: describe, explain, criticize

- ◆ **CRITICIZE** (to judge strong and weak points of something)
  - ▸ Make a list of the strong points and weak points

> ▸ Develop details, examples, and contrasts to support judgments
> ▸ Make an overall judgment of quality

♦ **EXPLAIN** (to show causes of or reasons for something)

> ▸ In Science, usually show the process that occurs in moving from one state or phase in a process to the next, thoroughly presenting details of each step
> ▸ In Humanities and often in Social Sciences, make a list of factors that influence something, developing evidence for each factor's potential influence

♦ **DESCRIBE** (to give major features of something)

> ▸ Pick out highlights or major aspects of something
> ▸ Develop details and illustrations to give a clear picture

♦ **ARGUE** (to give reasons for one position and against another)

> ▸ Make a list of reasons for the position
> ▸ Make a list of reasons against the position
> ▸ Refute objections to your reasons for and defend against objections to your reasons opposing the position
> ▸ Fill out reasons, objections, and replies with details, examples, consequences, and logical connections

♦ **COMMENT** (to make statements about something)

> ▸ Calls for a position, discussion, explanation, judgment, or evaluation regarding a subject, idea, or situation
> ▸ Is strengthened by providing supporting evidence, information, and examples

♦ **DEMONSTRATE** (to show something)

> ▸ Depending upon the nature of the subject matter, provide evidence, clarify the logical basis of something, appeal to principles or laws as in an explanation, supply a range of opinion and examples

♦ **SYNTHESIZE** (to invent a new or different version)

> ▸ Construct your own meaning based upon your knowledge and experiences
> ▸ Support your assertion with examples, references to literature and research studies

(Source: http://www.counc.ivic.ca/learn/program/hndouts/simple.html)

📖 TEST ANXIETY

Do you get test anxiety? Most students feel some level of stress, worry, or anxiety before an exam. Feeling a little tension or anxiety before or during an exam is normal for most students. A little stress or tension may help you rise to the challenge but too much stress or anxiety interferes with your ability to do well on the exam. Test anxiety may cause you to experience some of the following in a mild or more severe form:

- "butterflies" in your stomach, sweating, shortness of breath, or a quickened pulse
- disturbed sleep or eating patterns
- increased nervousness, fear, or irritability
- sense of hopelessness or panic
- drawing a "blank" during the exam

If you experience extreme forms of test anxiety you need to consult your family physician. For milder forms of anxiety you may find some of the following strategies effective in helping you to remain calm and focused during your unit tests or year-end exams.

- Acknowledge that you are feeling some stress or test anxiety and that this is normal
- Focus upon your breathing, taking several deep breaths
- Concentrate upon a single object for a few moments
- Tense and relax the muscles in areas of your body where you feel tension
- Break your exam into smaller, manageable, achievable parts
- Use positive self-talk to calm and motivate yourself. Tell yourself, "I can do this if I read carefully/start with the easy questions/focus on what I know/stick with it/. . ." instead of saying, "I can't do this."
- Visualize your successful completion of your review or the exam
- Recall a time in the past when you felt calm, relaxed, and content. Replay this experience in your mind experiencing it as fully as possible.

📖 *KEY* STRATEGIES FOR SUCCESS BEFORE AN EXAM – A CHECKLIST

Review, review, review. That's a huge part of your exam preparation. Here's a quick review checklist for you to see how many strategies for success you are using as you prepare to write your unit tests and year-end exams.

KEY Strategies for Success Before an Exam	*Yes*	*No*
Have you been attending classes?		
Have you determined your learning style?		
Have you organized a quiet study area for yourself?		
Have you developed a long-term study schedule?		
Have you developed a short-term study schedule?		
Are you working with a study buddy or study group?		
Is your study buddy/group positive, knowledgeable, motivated and supportive?		
Have you registered in tutorial classes?		
Have you developed your exam study notes?		
Have you reviewed previously administered exams?		
Have you practiced answering multiple choice, numerical response, written response, and essay questions?		
Have you analyzed the most common errors students make on each subject exam?		
Have you practiced strategies for controlling your exam anxiety?		
Have you maintained a healthy diet and sleep routine?		
Have you participated in regular physical activity?		

📖 *KEY* STRATEGIES FOR SUCCESS DURING AN EXAM

Doing well on any exam requires that you prepare in advance by reviewing your subject material and then using your knowledge to respond effectively to the exam questions during the test session. Combining subject knowledge with effective test writing skills gives you the best opportunity for success. The following are some strategies you may find useful in writing your exam.

- ◆ Managing Test Anxiety
  - ‣ Be as prepared as possible to increase your self-confidence.
  - ‣ Arrive at the exam on time and bring whatever materials you need to complete the exam such as pens, pencils, erasers, and calculators if they are allowed.
  - ‣ Drink enough water before you begin the exam so you are hydrated.
  - ‣ Associate with positive, calm individuals until you enter the exam room.
  - ‣ Use positive self-talk to calm yourself.
  - ‣ Remind yourself that it is normal to feel anxious about the exam.
  - ‣ Visualize your successful completion of the exam.
  - ‣ Breathe deeply several times.
  - ‣ Rotate your head, shrug your shoulders, and change positions to relax.

- ◆ While the information from your crib notes is still fresh in your memory, write down the key words, concepts, definitions, theories or formulas on the back of the test paper before you look at the exam questions.
  - ‣ Review the entire exam.
  - ‣ Budget your time.
  - ‣ Begin with the easiest question or the question that you know you can answer correctly rather than following the numerical question order of the exam.
  - ‣ Be aware of linked questions and use the clues to help you with other questions or in other parts of the exam.

If you "blank" on the exam, try repeating the deep breathing and physical relaxation activities first. Then move to visualization and positive self-talk to get you going. You can also try to open the 'information flow' by writing down anything that you remember about the subject on the reverse side of your exam paper. This activity sometimes helps you to remind yourself that you <u>do</u> know something and you are capable of writing the exam.

📖 GETTING STARTED

MANAGING YOUR TIME

- Plan on staying in the exam room for the full time that is available to you.

- Review the entire exam and calculate how much time you can spend on each section. Write your time schedule on the top of your paper and stick as closely as possible to the time you have allotted for each section of the exam.

- Be strategic and use your time where you will get the most marks. Avoid spending too much time on challenging questions that are not worth more marks than other questions that may be easier and are worth the same number of marks.

- If you are running short of time, switch to point form and write as much as you can for written response and essay questions so you have a chance of receiving partial marks.

- Leave time to review your paper asking yourself, "Did I do all of the questions I was supposed to do?", "Can I answer any questions now that I skipped over before?", "Are there any questions that I misinterpreted or misread?"

USING THE FIVE PASS METHOD

- **BROWSING STAGE** – Scan the entire exam noting the format, the specific instructions and marks allotted for each section, which questions you will complete and which ones you will omit if there is a choice.

- **THE FIRST ANSWERING PASS** – To gain confidence and momentum, answer only the questions you are confident you can answer correctly and quickly. These questions are most often found in the multiple choice or numerical response sections of the exam. Maintain a brisk pace; if a question is taking too long to answer, leave it for the Second or Third Pass.

- **THE SECOND ANSWERING PASS** – This Pass addresses questions which require more effort per mark. Answer as many of the remaining questions as possible while maintaining steady progress toward a solution. As soon as it becomes evident the question is too difficult or is tasking an inordinate amount of time, leave it for the Third Answering Pass.

- **THE THIRD ANSWERING PASS** – During the Third Answering Pass you should complete all partial solutions from the first two Passes. Marks are produced at a slower rate during this stage. At the end of this stage, all questions should have full or partial answers. Guess at any multiple choice questions that you have not yet answered.

- **THE FINAL REVIEW STAGE** – Use the remaining time to review the entire exam, making sure that no questions have been overlooked. Check answers and calculations as time permits.

USING THE THREE PASS METHOD

- **OVERVIEW** – Begin with an overview of the exam to see what it contains. Look for 'easy' questions and questions on topics that you know thoroughly.

- **SECOND PASS** – Answer all the questions that you can complete without too much trouble. These questions help to build your confidence and establish a positive start.

- **LAST PASS** – Now go through and answer the questions that are left. This is when you begin to try solving the questions you find particularly challenging.

📖 *KEY* EXAM TIPS FOR SELECTED SUBJECT AREAS

The following are a few additional suggestions you may wish to consider when writing exams in any of the selected subject areas.

ENGLISH LANGUAGE ARTS

Exams in English Language Arts usually have two components, writing and reading. Sometimes students are allowed to bring approved reference books such as a dictionary, thesaurus and writing handbook into the exam. If you have not used these references on a regular basis, you may find them more of a hindrance than a help in an exam situation. In completing the written section of an English Language Arts exam:

- plan your essay
- focus on the issue presented
- establish a clear position using a thesis statement to direct and unify your writing
- organize your writing in a manner that logically presents your views
- support your viewpoint with specific examples
- edit and proof read your writing

In completing the reading section of an English Language Arts exam:

- read the entire selection before responding
- use titles, dates, footnotes, pictures, introductions, and notes on the author to assist you in developing an understanding of the piece presented
- when using line references, read a few lines before and after the identified section

MATHEMATICS

In some instances, the use of calculators is permitted (or required) to complete complex calculations, modeling, simulations, or to demonstrate your use of technology. It is imperative that you are familiar with the approved calculator and the modes you may be using during your exam. In writing exams in mathematics:

- use appropriate mathematical notation and symbols

- clearly show or explain all the steps involved in solving the problem

- check to be sure you have included the correct units of measurement and have rounded to the appropriate significant digit

- use appropriate labelling and equal increments on graphs

SCIENCES

In the Sciences written response and open-ended questions usually require a clear, organized, and detailed explanation of the science involved in the question. You may find it helpful to use the acronym **STEEPLES** to organize your response to these types of questions. STEEPLES stands for **S**cience, **T**echnological, **E**cological, **E**thical, **P**olitical, **L**egal, **E**conomical, and **S**ocial aspects of the issue presented. In writing exams in the sciences:

- use scientific vocabulary to clearly explain your understanding of the processes or issues

- state your position in an objective manner

- demonstrate your understanding of both sides of the issue

- clearly label graphs, diagrams, tables, and charts using accepted conventions

- provide all formulas and equations

SOCIAL STUDIES, HISTORY, GEOGRAPHY

Exams in these courses of study often require you to take a position on an issue and defend your point of view. Your response should demonstrate your understanding of both the positive and negative aspects of the issue and be supported by well-considered arguments and evidence. In writing exams in Social Studies, History or Geography, the following acronyms may be helpful to you in organizing your approach.

- **SEE** – stands for **S**tatement, **E**xplanation, **E**xample. This acronym reminds you to couple your statement regarding your position with an explanation and then an example.

- **PERMS** – stands for **P**olitical, **E**conomic, **R**eligious or moral, **M**ilitary, and **S**ocietal values. Your position statement may be derived from or based upon any of these points of view. Your argument is more credible if you can show that recognized authorities such as leaders, theorists, writers or scientists back your position.

📖 SUMMARY

Writing exams involves a certain amount of stress and anxiety. If you want to do your best on the exam, *there is no substitute for being well prepared.* Being well prepared helps you to feel more confident about your ability to succeed and less anxious about writing tests. In preparing for unit or year-end exams remember to:

- use as many senses as possible in preparing for exams
- start as early as possible set realistic goals and targets
- take advantage of study buddies, study groups, and tutorials
- review previously used exams
- study with positive, knowledgeable, motivated, and supportive individuals
- practice the material in the format in which you are to be tested
- try to simulate the test situation as much as possible
- keep a positive attitude
- end your study time with a quick review and then do something different before you try to go to sleep on the night before the exam
- drink a sufficient amount of water prior to an exam
- stay in the exam room for the full amount of time available
- try to relax by focusing on your breathing

If you combine your best study habits with some of the strategies presented here, you may increase your chances of writing a strong exam and maximizing your potential to do well.

PRACTICE EXAMINATION

A GUIDE TO PREPARING FOR AN EXAMINATION

The questions presented here are distinct from those in the previous sections. **THE KEY** contains detailed answers that illustrate the problem-solving process for every question in this section.

Students are encouraged to write this practice exam under conditions similar to those they will encounter when writing their final exam. This will make students:

- *aware of the mental and physical stamina required to sit through an entire exam*
- *familiar with the exam format and how the course content is tested*
- *aware of any units or concepts that are troublesome or require additional study*
- *more successful in managing their review effectively*

To simulate the exam conditions students should:

- *use an alarm clock or other timer to monitor the time allowed for the exam*
- *select a quiet writing spot away from all distractions*
- *assemble the appropriate materials that are allowed for writing the exam such as pens, HB pencils, calculator, dictionary*
- *use "test wiseness" skills*
- *complete as much of the exam as possible within the allowable time*

In writing the practice exam students should:

- *read instructions, directions and questions carefully*
- *organize writing time according to the exam emphasis on each section*
- *highlight key words*
- *think about what is being asked*
- *plan their writing; once complete, proof for errors in content, spelling, grammar*
- *watch for bolded words such as most, least, best*
- *in Multiple Choice questions, cross out any choices students know are incorrect*
- *if possible, review all responses upon completion of the exam*

NOTES

PRACTICE EXAMINATION

READING ONE

Catherine Morland, the protagonist of Jane Austen's Northanger Abbey, *is unfit for her role as a heroine. The reason for her unsuitability is found in the nature of the Gothic romances that were popular at the time. The Gothic genre required a heroine to possess remarkable beauty and unusual abilities. She would also be expected to endure grotesque and horrible events, supernatural horrors, and isolation in a ruinous castle or an abbey (a monastery). She would be caught up in dark secrets or the results of ancient crimes, and she might find an evil monk or nun adding to the darkness and gloom. The Gothic genre also required brooding, tyrannical male characters that might include a harsh and unreasonable father or an eligible bachelor with a tortured past. All of these Gothic elements, and Catherine's lack thereof, make her an unlikely heroine.*

from NORTHANGER ABBEY

No one who had ever seen Catherine Morland in her infancy would have supposed her born to be a heroine. Her situation in life, the character of her father and mother, her own person[1] and disposition, were all equally against her. Her father was a clergyman, without being neglected, or poor, and a very respectable man, though his name was Richard – and he had never been handsome. He had a

5 considerable independence[2] besides two good livings[3] – and he was not in the least addicted to locking up his daughters. Her mother was a woman of useful plain sense, with a good temper, and, what is more remarkable, with a good constitution. She had three sons before Catherine was born; and instead of dying in bringing the latter into the world, as anybody might expect, she still lived on – lived to have six children more – to see them growing up and around her, and to enjoy excellent health herself.

10 A family of ten children will be always called a fine family, where there are heads and arms and legs enough for the number; but the Morlands had little other right to the word, for they were in general very plain, and Catherine, for many years of her life, as plain as any. She had a thin awkward figure, a sallow skin without colour, dark lank hair, and strong features – so much for her person; and not less unpropitious for heroism seemed her mind. She was fond of all boys' plays, and greatly preferred cricket

15 not merely to dolls, but to the more heroic enjoyments of infancy, nursing a dormouse, feeding a canary-bird, or watering a rose-bush. Indeed she had no taste for a garden; and if she gathered flowers at

---

[1] person – appearance, looks

[2] independence – an income from invested money

[3] living – the property owners in a parish had to pay to support the local church (parish). The yearly income from a parish was called a *living*. Some Anglican clergymen received the income from more than one parish. (Many clergymen were quite poor, however.)

all, it was chiefly for the pleasure of mischief – at least so it was conjectured from her always preferring those which she was forbidden to take. Such were her propensities – her abilities were quite as extraordinary. She never could learn or understand anything before she was taught; and sometimes not

20 even then, for she was often inattentive, and occasionally stupid. Her mother was three months in teaching her only to repeat the "Beggar's Petition"; and after all, her next sister, Sally, could say it better than she did. Not that Catherine was always stupid – by no means; she learnt the fable of "the Hare and Many Friends"[4] as quickly as any girl in England.

Her mother wished her to learn music; and Catherine was sure she should like it, for she was very fond of

25 tinkling the keys of the old forlorn spinet;[5] so, at eight years old she began. She learnt a year, and could not bear it; and Mrs. Morland, who did not insist on her daughters being accomplished in spite of incapacity or distaste, allowed her to leave off. The day which dismissed the music-master was one of the happiest of Catherine's life. Her taste for drawing was not superior; though whenever she could obtain the outside of a letter from her mother or seize upon any other odd piece of paper, she did what she could

30 in that way, by drawing houses and trees, hens and chickens, all very much like one another. Writing and accounts she was taught by her father; French by her mother. Her proficiency in either was not remarkable, and she shirked her lessons in both whenever she could.

What a strange, unaccountable character! – for with all these symptoms of profligacy at ten years old, she had neither a bad heart nor a bad temper, was seldom stubborn, scarcely ever quarrelsome, and very kind

35 to the little ones, with few interruptions of tyranny. She was, moreover, noisy and wild, hated confinement and cleanliness, and loved nothing so well in the world as rolling down the green slope at the back of the house.

Such was Catherine Morland at ten. At fifteen, appearances were mending; she began to curl her hair and long for balls; her complexion improved, her features were softened by plumpness and colour, her eyes

40 gained more animation, and her figure more consequence. Her love of dirt gave way to an inclination for finery, and she grew clean as she grew smart; she had now the pleasure of sometimes hearing her father and mother remark on her personal improvement. "Catherine grows quite a good-looking girl – she is almost pretty today," were words which caught her ears now and then; and how welcome were the sounds! To look *almost* pretty is an acquisition of higher delight to a girl who has been looking plain the

45 first fifteen years of her life than a beauty from her cradle can ever receive.

Mrs. Morland was a very good woman, and wished to see her children everything they ought to be; but her time was so much occupied in lying-in and teaching the little ones, that her elder daughters were

---

[4] "Hare and Many Friends"—a relatively light-hearted animal fable and only half as long as "Petition," which is a grim social commentary about starvation.

[5] spinet – a simple harpsichord (a piano-like instrument); spinet is the modern spelling

inevitably left to shift for themselves; and it was not very wonderful that Catherine, who had by nature

nothing heroic about her, should prefer cricket, baseball, riding on horseback, and running about the

50 country at the age of fourteen, to books – or at least books of information – for, provided that nothing like

useful knowledge could be gained from them, provided they were all story an no reflection, she had never

any objection to books at all. But from fifteen to seventeen she was in training for a heroine; she read all

such works as heroines must read to supply their memories with those quotations which are so serviceable

and so soothing in the vicissitudes[6] of their eventful lives.

55 From Pope,[7] she learnt to censure those who

"bear about the mockery of woe."

From Gray, that

"Many a flower is born to blush unseen,

And waste its sweetness on the desert air."

60 From Thompson, that –

"It is a delightful task

To teach the young idea how to shoot."[8]

And from Shakespeare she gained a great store of information – amongst the rest, that –

"Trifles light as air,

65   Are, to the jealous, confirmation strong,

As proofs of Holy Writ."

That

"The poor beetle, which we tread upon,

In corporal sufferance feels a pang as great

70   As when a giant dies."

And that a young woman in love always looks –

"like Patience on a monument,

Smiling at Grief."

So far her improvement was sufficient – and in many other points she came on exceedingly well; for

75 though she could not write sonnets, she brought herself to read them; and though there seemed no chance

---

[6] vicissitudes – unexpected changes in fortune

[7] Pope, Gray, Thompson, and Shakespeare all wrote love-poetry

[8] shoot – grow

of her throwing a whole party into raptures by a prelude on the pianoforte[9] of her own composition, she could listen to other people's performance with very little fatigue. Her greatest deficiency was in the pencil – she had no notion of drawing – not enough even to attempt a sketch of her lover's profile, that she might be detected in the design. There she fell miserably short of the true heroic height. At present

80 she did not know her own poverty, for she had no lover[10] to portray. She had reached the age of seventeen, without having seen one amiable youth who could call forth her sensibility, without having inspired one real passion, and without having excited even any admiration but what was very moderate and very transient. This was strange indeed! But strange things may be generally accounted for if their cause be fairly searched out. There was not one lord in the neighbourhood; no – not even a baronet.

85 There was not one family among their acquaintance who had reared and supported a boy accidentally found at their door – not one young man whose origin was unknown. Her father had no ward, and the squire of the parish no children. But when a young lady is to be a heroine, the perverseness of forty surrounding families cannot prevent her. Something must and will happen to throw a hero in her way.

Mr. Allen, who owned the chief of the property about Fullerton, the village in Wiltshire where the

90 Morlands lived, was ordered to Bath for the benefit of a gouty constitution – and his lady, a good-humoured woman, fond of Miss Morland, and probably aware that if adventures will not befall a young lady in her own village, she must seek them abroad, invited her to go with them. Mr. and Mrs. Morland were all compliance, and Catherine all happiness.

Jane Austen (1775–1817)
An English novelist, Austen wrote
her elegant and realistic novels of manners at a time
when sensational and improbable Gothic romances were popular.

---

[9] pianoforte – piano

[10] lover – beloved; one who loves or is loved (before the 1900s, no further meaning need be assumed)

1. Which of the following quotations **most directly** explains the narrator's surprise that Catherine Morland is the heroine of this story?

    A. "Her father was a clergyman, without being neglected, or poor, and a very respectable man, though his name was Richard – and he had never been handsome" (lines 3–4)

    B. "Her mother wished her to learn music…She learnt a year, and could not bear it; and Mrs. Morland, who did not insist on her daughters being accomplished in spite of incapacity or distaste, allowed her to leave off" (lines 24–27)

    C. "Writing and accounts she was taught be her father, French by her mother; her proficiency in either was not remarkable, and she shirked her lessons in both whenever she could" (lines 30–32)

    D. "She was, moreover, noisy and wild, hated confinement and cleanliness, and loved nothing so well in the world as rolling down the green slope at the back of the house". (lines 35–37)

2. The word "propensities" (line 18) most likely means

    A. ideas

    B. skills

    C. abilities

    D. inclinations

3. At ten years of age, Catherine still does not seem to be much of a heroine because, according to the narrator,

    A. her mother "had three sons before Catherine was born" (line 7)

    B. "The day which dismissed her music master was one of the happiest of Catherine's life" (lines 27–28)

    C. "she shirked her lessons…whenever she could" (line 32)

    D. "she had neither a bad heart nor a bad temper" (lines 33–34)

4. The description of Catherine as "a strange, unaccountable character!" (line 33) is **most clearly** explained as

   A. irony that shows she was perfectly normal

   B. metaphor that shows she was an awkward ten-year-old

   C. parody that shows the narrator is easily surprised by her

   D. metonymy that shows she did really have a bad character after all

5. The **most complete** description of Catherine's "propensities" and "abilities" is that they are

   A. described in terms of what she cannot do

   B. quite remarkable for someone so young

   C. focused on heroic deeds in the future

   D. more mischievous than anything else

6. From this introduction to Catherine, it is **most likely** that the rest of the story will

   A. show how she deserves to be called a heroine

   B. continue to tell how ordinary she is

   C. describe the rest of her family

   D. give her complete biography

7. The **best** description of the narrator's tone in this passage is

   A. ironic

   B. Gothic

   C. derisive

   D. insincere

8. In the context of lines 79 to 83, "sensibility" **most clearly** means

   A. feelings

   B. admiration

   C. social rank

   D. common sense

9. This excerpt is really about the

    A. importance of education

    B. qualities necessary for heroism

    C. foolishness of certain kinds of stories

    D. unequal education given to girls in the 1800s

10. The genre of this extract may be **most accurately** described as

    A. burlesque

    B. romance

    C. parody

    D. Gothic

READING TWO

FROM PLATO'S REPUBLIC

In this excerpt from one of the dialogues recorded by the Greek philosopher Plato, Socrates (the "I")
tells of speaking with Glaucon (the "he") about the human situation. The brief replies made by Glaucon
are typical of a Socratic dialogue. The dialectic teaching method of question and answer is called the
Socratic method.

The Myth of the Cave

And now, I said, let me show in a figure how far our nature is enlightened or unenlightened: – Behold!
Human beings living in an underground den, which has a mouth open toward the light and reaching all
along the den; here they have been from their childhood, and have their legs and necks chained so that
they cannot move, and can only see before them, being prevented by the chains from turning round their
5 heads. Above and behind them a fire is blazing at a distance, and between the fire and the prisoners there
is a raised way;[1] and you will see, if you look, a low wall built along the way, like the screen which
marionette players have in front of them, over which they show the puppets.

I see.

And do you see, I said, men[2] passing along the wall carrying all sorts of vessels, and statues and figures of
10 animals made of wood and stone and various materials, which appear over the wall? Some of them are
talking, others silent.

You have shown me a strange image, and they are strange prisoners.

Like ourselves, I replied; and they see only their own shadows, or the shadows of one another, which the
fire throws on the opposite wall of the cave?

15 True, he said; how could they see anything but the shadows if they were never allowed to move their
heads?

And of the objects which are being carried in like manner they would only see the shadows?

Yes, he said.

And if they were able to converse with one another, would they not suppose that they were naming what
20 was actually before them?

Very true.

---

[1] way – road or path
[2] men – people, human beings

And suppose further that the prison had an echo which came from the other side, would they not be sure to fancy when one of the passers-by spoke that the voice which they heard came from the passing shadow?

25 No question, he replied.

To them, I said, the truth would be literally nothing but the shadows of the images.

That is certain.

And now look again, and see what will naturally follow if the prisoners are released and disabused of their error. At first, when any of them is liberated and compelled suddenly to stand up and turn his neck
30 round and walk and look toward the light, he will suffer sharp pains; the glare will distress him, and he will be unable to see the realities of which in his former state he had seen the shadows; and then conceive someone saying to him, that what he saw before was an illusion, but that now, when he is approaching nearer to being and his eye is turned toward more real existence, he has a clearer vision – what will be his reply? And you may further imagine that his instructor is pointing to the objects as they pass and
35 requiring him to name them – will he not be perplexed? Will he not fancy that the shadows which he formerly saw are truer than the objects which are now shown to him?

Far truer.

And if he is compelled to look straight at the light, will he not have a pain in his eyes which will make him turn away to take refuge in the objects of vision which he can see, and which he will conceive to be
40 in reality clearer than the things which are now being shown to him?

True, he said.

And suppose once more, that he is reluctantly dragged up a steep and rugged ascent, and held fast until he is forced into the presence of the sun himself, is he not likely to be pained and irritated? When he approaches the light his eyes will be dazzled, and he will not be able to see anything at all of what are
45 now called realities.

Not all in a moment, he said.

He will require to grow accustomed to the sight of the upper world. And first he will see the shadows best, next the reflections of men and other objects in the water, and then the objects themselves; then he will gaze upon the light of the moon and the stars and the spangled heaven; and he will see the sky and
50 the stars by night better than the sun or the light of the sun by day?

Certainly.

Last of all he will be able to see the sun, and not mere reflections of him in the water, but he will see him in his own proper place, and not in another; and he will contemplate him as he is.

Certainly.

55 He will then proceed to argue that this is he who gives the season and the years, and is the guardian of all

   that is in the visible world, and in a certain way the cause of all things which he and his fellows have been

   accustomed to behold?

   Clearly, he said, he would first see the sun and then reason about him.

   And when he remembered his old habitation, and the wisdom of the den and his fellow-prisoners, do you

60 not suppose that he would felicitate himself on the change, and pity them?

   Certainly, he would.

   And if they were in the habit of conferring honours among themselves on those who were quickest to

   observe the passing shadows and to remark which of them went before, and which followed after, and

   which were together; and who were therefore best able to draw conclusions as to the future, do you think

65 that he would care for such honours and glories, or envy the possessors of them? Would he not say with

   Homer,[3]

> Better to be the poor servant of a poor master, and to endure anything, rather than think as they
> do and live after their manner?

   Yes, he said, I think that he would rather suffer anything than entertain these false notions and live in this

70 miserable manner.

   Imagine once more, I said, such a one coming suddenly out of the sun to be replaced in his old situation;

   would he not be certain to have his eyes full of darkness?

   To be sure, he said.

   And if there were a contest, and he had to compete in measuring the shadows with the prisoners who had

75 never moved out of the den, while his sight was still weak, and before his eyes had become steady (and

   the time which would be needed to acquire this new habit of sight might be very considerable) would he

   not be ridiculous? Men would say of him that up he went and down he came without his eyes; and that it

   was better not even to think of ascending; and if anyone tried to loose another and lead him up to the

   light, let them only catch the offender, and they would put him to death.

80 No question, he said.

   This entire allegory, I said, you may now append,[4] dear Glaucon, to the previous argument;[5] the

   prison-house is the world of sight, the light of the fire is the sun, and you will not misapprehend me if you

   interpret the journey upwards to be the ascent of the soul into the intellectual world according to my poor

---

[3] Homer (8th or 9th century BC) – Greek poet; author of the Iliad and the Odyssey; allusions to his work were
frequent in classical Greece
[4] append – add to
[5] previous argument – this extract does not include all of the conversation between Socrates and Glaucon.

belief, which, at your desire, I have expressed whether rightly or wrongly, God knows. But, whether true
85 or false, my opinion is that in the world of knowledge the idea of good appears last of all, and is seen only
with an effort; and, when seen, is also inferred to be the universal author of all things beautiful and right,
parent of light and of the lord of light in this visible world, and the immediate source of reason and truth
in the intellectual; and that this is the power upon which he who would act rationally either in public or
private life must have his eye fixed.

Plato (427–347 BC)
Most of what we know about the ideas of
Socrates (469–399 BC) is found in the writings of Plato

11. Which of the following quotations **most strongly** presents the theme of limited perception?

A. "Behold! Human beings living in an underground den, which has a mouth open toward
the light and reaching all along the den" (lines 1–3)

B. "here they have been from their childhood, and have their legs and necks chained to that
they cannot move, and can only see before them, being prevented by the chains from
turning round their heads" (lines 3–5)

C. "and you will see, if you look, a low all built along the way like the screen which
marionette players have in front of them, over which they show the puppets" (lines 6–7)

D. "And do you see, I said, men passing along the wall carrying all sorts of vessels, and
statues and figures of animals made of wood and stone and various materials, which
appear over the wall?" (lines 9–10)

12. According to Socrates, the liberated prisoner will paradoxically

A. regret his liberation

B. throw caution to the wind

C. have to be forced to leave the prison

D. experience more intense levels of pain

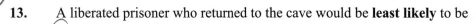

13. A liberated prisoner who returned to the cave would be **least likely** to be

    A. put to death

    B. seen to be ridiculous

    C. unable to see as well as the others

    D. at a disadvantage compared to those who had never left

14. In this context, the **main** function of a "myth" such as the one told by Socrates is to

    A. express a truth about the human condition

    B. make a vivid image which the reader can "see"

    C. state in images a thought that is too difficult for ordinary words

    D. briefly summarize a moral principle that is sometimes stated at the end of a story

15. The first paragraph explains that through this myth, the writer will show "how far our nature is enlightened or unenlightened," and then goes on to posit that man is

    A. unenlightened because of the immobilizing chains

    B. enlightened because of the "fire blazing at a distance"

    C. unenlightened because of external causes beyond our control

    D. both enlightened and unenlightened because of the shadows cast by the fire

16. The function of the dialogue in the telling of this myth is **best** summarized as a way

    A. to simplify a complicated story

    B. for the reader to infer the meaning of the argument

    C. of teaching by proceeding one step at a time through question and answer

    D. to provide a "yes-man" that will cause unconscious agreement with the argument

17. The narrator's overall attitude toward human nature is **best** stated as

    A. cynical

    B. realistic

    C. optimistic

    D. pessimistic

18. In the analogy of the myth, the location that is **most** real is

    A. "an underground den" (line 2)

    B. the fire which is blazing "above and behind" them (line 5)

    C. the other side of "a low wall built along the way" (line 6)

    D. "the shadows of the images" (line 26)

19. The meaning of the phrase "show in a figure" (line 1) is **most clearly** explained as

    A. a shadow play

    B. a figure of speech

    C. the result of calculation

    D. an illustration that demonstrates truth

20. In lines 88 to 89, Socrates is saying that anyone who wants to behave rationally should

    A. be guided by the light of the sun

    B. remember that the world is a prison

    C. understand that nothing that we see is really true

    D. remember that good is the source of truth in everything

21. According to Socrates, truth is understood through

    A. inference

    B. figures of speech

    C. studying shadows

    D. the light of the sun

READING THREE

CROSSING THE BAR

Sunset and evening star,

And one clear call for me!

And may there be no moaning of the bar,[1]

When I put out to sea,

5   But such a tide as moving seems asleep,

Too full for sound and foam,

When that which drew from out the boundless deep

Turns again home.

Twilight and evening bell,

10 And after that the dark!

And may there be no sadness of farewell,

When I embark;

For though from out our bourne[2] of Time and Place

The flood may bear me far,

15 I hope to see my Pilot[3] face to face

When I have crossed the bar.

Alfred, Lord Tennyson (1809–92)
Tennyson was one of the best-known Victorian
poets. He requested that "Crossing the Bar" always
be the last poem printed in any collection of his works.

---

[1] bar – low ridge of gravel at the mouth of a harbour; it is near the surface and may be exposed at low tide
[2] bourne – boundary between one place and another
[3] pilot – sailor with local knowledge who guides a ship through a difficult or dangerous stretch of water

22. The theme of this poem is **best** described as the

    A.   inevitable

    B.   silence of eternity

    C.   approach of death

    D.   acceptance of death

23. The phrase "moaning of the bar" is **best** explained as

    A.   weeping

    B.   suffering

    C.   ship-board noises

    D.   the rush of the tide over gravel

24. In line 15, "my Pilot" **most likely** refers to

    A.   God

    B.   eternity

    C.   the ship's guide

    D.   someone who can show the way

25. Which of the following quotations **most clearly** expresses the poet's attitude?

    A.   "Twilight and evening bell, / And after that the dark!" (lines 9–10)

    B.   "When that which drew from out the boundless deep / Turns again home" (lines 7–8)

    C.   "But such a tide as moving seems asleep" (line 5)

    D.   "And may there be no moaning of the bar, / When I put out to sea" (lines 3–4)

26. In lines 13 and 15, three words other than the first words of each line are capitalized because

   A.   of poetic licence

   B.   proper nouns are always capitalized

   C.   of their importance in the poet's thought

   D.   in Tennyson's day, English had different rules for capitalization

27. In the quotation "When that which drew from out the boundless deep" (line 7), the pronoun "that" does not have a clear antecedent—it might not even refer to anything mentioned before. The antecedent of the pronoun "that" is the

   A.   "I" (line 12) who is embarking on a journey

   B.   tide that moves to and from "the boundless deep"

   C.   soul leaving the boundary of time and space (line 13)

   D.   Pilot (line 15) who guides the ship once it has left harbour

28. The tone of this poem is **best described** as

   A.   calm

   B.   anxious

   C.   grieving

   D.   hopeless

READING FOUR

from THE TEMPEST, ACT III, SCENE III

CHARACTERS

ALONSO, King of Naples

SEBASTIAN, his brother

PROSPERO, the right Duke of Milan

ANTONIO, his brother, the usurping Duke of Milan

FERDINAND, son to the King of Naples

MIRANDA, daughter to Prospero

GONZALO, an honest old Counsellor

ADRIAN, FRANCISCO, Lords

ARIEL, an airy spirit

On an almost uninhabited island somewhere in the Mediterranean Sea, Prospero lives with his daughter Miranda. Prospero, who has become a powerful magician, is also the rightful Duke of Milan. Twelve years ago, Prospero's brother Antonio, with the help of Alonso, the King of Naples, seized Milan. Antonio and Alonso conspired to have Prospero and the infant Miranda, whom they dared not murder outright, put out to sea in a leaky boat to drown. However, the two castaways did not drown, partly because Gonzalo, one of Alonso's lords, secretly provided them with supplies as well as books—including the all-important book of magic—from Prospero's library.

Over the next twelve years, Prospero's power has grown and he now has powerful spirits of the air for his servants. When Antonio, Alonso, and others of their courts pass near the island on ship, Prospero arranges a great storm and an apparent shipwreck. He now has them all in his power.

As this scene begins, the characters, confused by magic, have been wandering in circles for some time.

Enter ALONSO, SEBASTIAN, ANTONIO, GONZALO, ADRIAN, FRANCISCO, and others.

GONZALO: By'r lakin,[1] I can go no further, sir;

My old bones ache: here's a maze trod indeed

Through forth-rights and meanders![2] By your patience,

5   I needs must rest me.

---

[1] By'r lakin – an oath or exclamation; a worn-down form of By Our Lady
[2] forth-rights and meanders – straight and crooked paths

ALONSO: Old lord, I cannot blame thee,

Who am myself attach'd with weariness,

To the dulling of my spirits: sit down, and rest.

Even here I will put off my hope and keep it

10 No longer for my flatterer: he is drown'd

Whom thus we stray to find, and the sea mocks

Our frustrate search on land. Well, let him go.

ANTONIO: *[Aside to* SEBASTIAN*]* I am right glad that he's so out of hope.

Do not, for one repulse,[3] forego the purpose

15 That you resolved to effect.

SEBASTIAN: *[Aside to* ANTONIO*]* The next advantage

Will we take throughly.[4]

ANTONIO: *[Aside to SEBASTIAN]* Let it be to-night;

For, now they are oppress'd with travel, they

20 Will not, nor cannot, use such vigilance

As when they are fresh.

SEBASTIAN: *[Aside to ANTONIO]* I say, to-night: no more.

[Solemn and strange music]

ALONSO: What harmony is this? My good friends, hark!

25 **GONZALO:** Marvellous sweet music!

Enter PROSPERO above, invisible. Enter several strange Shapes, bringing in a banquet; they dance about it with gentle actions of salutation; and, inviting the King, etc. to eat, they depart

ALONSO: Give us kind keepers, heavens! What were these?

SEBASTIAN: A living drollery.[5] Now I will believe

30 That there are unicorns, that in Arabia

There is one tree, the phoenix' throne, one phoenix

At this hour reigning there.

ANTONIO: I'll believe both;

---

[3] repulse – setback
[4] throughly – thoroughly
[5] drollery – comic show

And what does else want credit, come to me,

35   And I'll be sworn 'tis true: travelers ne'er did lie,

Though fools at home condemn 'em.

GONZALO: If in Naples

I should report this now, would they believe me?

If I should say, I saw such islanders –

40   For, certes, these are people of the island –

Who, though they are of monstrous shape, yet, note,

Their manners are more gentle-kind than of

Our human generation you shall find

Many, nay, almost any.

45   **PROSPERO:** *[Aside]* Honest lord,

Thou hast said well; for some of you there present

Are worse than devils.

ALONSO: I cannot too much muse

Such shapes, such gesture and such sound, expressing,

50   Although they want the use of tongue, a kind

Of excellent dumb discourse.

PROSPERO: *[Aside]* Praise in departing.[6]

FRANCISCO: They vanish'd strangely.

SEBASTIAN: No matter, since

55   they have left their viands behind; for we have stomachs.

Will't please you taste of what is here?

ALONSO: Not I.

GONZALO: Faith, sir, you need not fear. When we were boys,

Who would believe that there were mountaineers

60   Dew-lapp'd like bulls, whose throats[7] had hanging at 'em

Wallets of flesh? or that there were such men

---

[6] Praise in departing – save your applause until the end

[7] throats – allusions to fantastic travellers' tales; the reference to *throats* is, in fact, a true tale: a thyroid disorder
       causes such swellings in the neck

Whose heads stood in their breasts? which we now find

Each putter-out of five for one[8] will bring us

Good warrant of.

65   **ALONSO:**   I will stand to and feed,

Although my last: no matter, since I feel

The best is past. Brother, my lord the duke,

Stand to and do as we.

Thunder and lightning. Enter ARIEL, *like a harpy;[9] claps his wings upon the table; and, with a quaint*

70   *device, the banquet vanishes.*

  ARIEL: You are three men of sin, whom Destiny –

That hath to instrument this lower world

And what is in't – the never-surfeited sea

Hath caused to belch up you; and on this island

75   Where man doth not inhabit; you 'mongst men

Being most unfit to live. I have made you mad;

And even with such-like valour men hang and drown
Their proper selves.

[ALONSO, SEBASTIAN, etc. draw their swords]

80   You fools! I and my fellows

Are ministers of Fate: the elements,

Of whom your swords are temper'd, may as well

Wound the loud winds, or with bemock'd-at stabs

Kill the still-closing waters, as diminish

85   One dowle that's in my plume: my fellow-ministers

Are like invulnerable. If you could hurt,

Your swords are not too massy for your strengths

And will not be uplifted. But remember –

For that's my business to you – that you three

90   From Milan did supplant good Prospero;

---

[8] putter-out of five for one – traveller who has taken out insurance (at five to one)

[9] *harpy* – in Greek mythology, harpies were monstrous birds with women's faces sent by Zeus to punish King Phineus by stealing the food from his table and fouling whatever crumbs were left

Exposed unto the sea, which hath requit it,

Him and his innocent child: for which foul deed

The powers, delaying, not forgetting, have

Incensed the seas and shores, yea, all the creatures,

95   Against your peace. Thee of thy son, Alonso,

They have bereft; and do pronounce by me

Lingering perdition,[10] worse than any death

Can be at once, shall step by step attend

You and your ways; whose wraths to guard you from –

100   Which here, in this most desolate isle, else falls

Upon your heads – is nothing but heart-sorrow

And a clear life ensuing.

He vanishes in thunder; then, to soft music enter the Shapes again, and dance, with mocks and mows, and carrying out the table.

105   **PROSPERO:** Bravely the figure of this harpy hast thou

Perform'd, my Ariel; a grace it had, devouring:

Of my instruction hast though nothing bated

In what thou hadst to say: so, with good life

And observation strange, my meaner ministers

110   Their several kinds have done. My high charms work

And these mine enemies are all knit up

In their distractions; they now are in my power;

And in these fits I leave them, while I visit

Young Ferdinand, whom they suppose is drown'd,

115   And his and mind loved darling.

[Exit above]

GONZALO: I' the name of something holy, sir, why stand you

In this strange stare?

ALONSO: O, it is monstrous, monstrous:

---

[10] perdition – damnation

120 Methought the billows spoke and told me of it;

The winds did sing it to me, and the thunder,

That deep and dreadful organ-pipe, pronounced

The name of Prosper: it did bass[11] my trespass.

Therefore my son i' the ooze is bedded, and

125 I'll seek him deeper than e'er plummet sounded

And with him there lie mudded.

[Exit]

SEBASTIAN: But one fiend at a time,

I'll fight their legions o'er.

130 **ANTONIO:** I'll be thy second.

[Exeunt[12] SEBASTIAN, and ANTONIO]

GONZALO: All three of them are desperate: their great guilt,

Like poison given to work a great time after,

Now 'gins to bite the spirits. I do beseech you

135 that are of suppler joints, follow them swiftly

And hinder them from what this ecstasy

May now provoke them to.

ADRIAN: Follow, I pray you.

[Exeunt]

29. Line 33 begins with only a few words printed at the end of the line that contains the character's name. The **most likely** reason for this is that

    A. the space contained directions that are not needed in this short excerpt

    B. the short line completes the iambic pentameter begun by the previous speaker

    C. many of the lines vary in length and the short lines actually have no significance

    D. the short first line is a poetic device intended to give relief from the monotonous rhythm

---

[11] bass – notice how the noun is used as an unusual verb and as a part of a figure of speech

[12] Exeunt – exit; a stage direction used when more than one actor leaves the stage

30. Gonzalo's words "here's a maze trod indeed / Through forth-rights and meanders!" (lines 3 to 4) are an example of

   A. a figure of speech

   B. dramatic poetry

   C. scene-setting

   D. metaphor

31. At the beginning of the scene, Antonio says, "I am right glad that he's so out of hope" (line 13). By "out of hope", Antonio means that Alonso

   A. is weakened by exhaustion

   B. feels trapped on the island

   C. is troubled by remorse

   D. thinks his son is dead

32. Sebastian's quotation, "A living drollery. Now I will believe / That there are unicorns, that in Arabia / There is one tree, the phoenix' throne, one phoenix / At this hour reigning there" (lines 29 to 32), contains examples of

   A. allusion

   B. metaphor

   C. metonymy

   D. synecdoche

33. After his speech in lines 119 – 126, Alonso exits in order to

   A. look for his missing son

   B. flee from his guilt

   C. fight the fiends

   D. seek death

34. Ariel appearing like a harpy and making the food vanish suggests

    A.   the hunger of the shipwrecked men

    B.   an allusion to classical mythology

    C.   a punishment for crime

    D.   increasing horror

35. In lines 117 to 118, Gonzalo says to Alonzo, "I' the name of something holy, sir, why stand you / In this strange stare?" because

    A.   he is trying to stir Alonzo out of his strange mood

    B.   Alonzo is on the point of confessing his crime

    C.   only the three guilty ones heard and saw Ariel

    D.   he is concerned for Alonso's sanity

36. Which of the following quotations **best** show Alonso's guilty feelings?

    A.   "Even here I will put off my hope and keep it / No longer for my flatterer" (lines 9–10)

    B.   "the sea mocks / Our frustrate search on land. Well, let him go" (lines 11–12)

    C.   "no matter, since I feel / The best is past" (lines 66–67)

    D.   "That deep and dreadful organ-pipe, pronounced / The name of Prosper; it did bass my trespass" (lines 122 – 123)

37. When Gonzalo uses the word "ecstasy" in line 136, he means

    A.   intense feeling or activity

    B.   loss of self-control

    C.   spiritual uplifting

    D.   intense delight

READING FIVE

from DEACON BRODIE, OR THE DOUBLE LIFE: A MELODRAMA IN FIVE ACTS AND EIGHT TABLEAUX

he Wrights, housebreaker and master carpenter

er

r-Fiscal,[1] the Deacon's uncle

sister

BLEAUX

uble Life

he Runner

r Clarke's

nd Good

Evidence

ked

obbery

Open Door

nd, a public prosecutor and coroner

William Brodie (1741–88) actually lived in Edinburgh, Scotland, and was Deacon of Wrights (Head of the Guild of Master Carpenters). He was a very respectable and prosperous citizen, but he led a secret double life: he gambled and lost heavily, kept two mistresses and had five children by them, and he used his craftsman's skills to burgle the houses of his fellow tradesmen. According to legend, he was the first criminal to be hanged on the new kind of gallows that he himself had designed and built.

The Stage represents a room in the Deacon's house, furnished partly as a sittingroom, partly as a bedroom, in the style of an easy burgess of about 1780. C.,[2] a door; L. C., a second and smaller door; R. C., practicable window; L., alcove, supposed to contain a bed; at the back, a clothes-press and a corner cupboard containing bottles, etc. MARY BRODIE at needlework; OLD BRODIE, a paralytic,[3] in a

5 wheeled chair, at the fireside, L.

SCENE I

To these LESLIE, C.

LESLIE: May I come in, Mary?

MARY: Why not?

10 **LESLIE:** I scarce knew where to find you.

MARY: The dad and I must have a corner, must we not? So when my brother's friends are in the parlour he allows us to sit in his room: 'Tis a great favour, I can tell you; the place is sacred.

LESLIE: Are you sure that 'sacred' is strong enough?

MARY: You are satirical!

15 **LESLIE:** I? And with regard to the Deacon? Believe me, I am not so ill-advised: You have trained me well, and I feel by him as solemnly as a true-born Brodie.

MARY: And now you are impertinent! Do you mean to go any further? We are a fighting race, we Brodies: Oh, you may laugh, sir! But 'tis no child's play to jest us on our Deacon, or, for that matter, on our Deacon's chamber either: It was his father's before him: he works in it by day and sleeps in it by

20 night; and scarce anything it contains but is that labour of his hands: Do you see this table, Walter? He made it while he was yet a 'prentice: I remember how I used to sit and watch him at his work: It would be grand, I thought, to be able to do as he did, and handle edge-tools without cutting my fingers, and getting my ears pulled for a meddlesome minx! He used to give me his mallet to keep and his nails to hold; and didn't I fly when he called for them! And wasn't I proud to be ordered about with them! And then, you

---

[2] C – stage direction indicating centre of the stage; also L (left) and R (right) centre; not the old-fashioned working of some of the directions.

[3] paralytic – someone paralyzed by stroke

Faculty of

SCIENCE

University of Alberta

**Your science
career begins
at the U of A
Faculty of Science**

With close to 60 degrees in over 40 subject areas,
the Faculty of Science at the U of A offers some
of the best undergraduate Science programs in
North America. Our Faculty is internationally
recognized for its teaching and research
excellence – **Explore what we have to offer!**

CW 223 Biological Sciences Building

University of Alberta

Edmonton, Alberta T6G 2E9

Tel: (780) 492-4758

E-mail: dean.science@ualberta.ca

www.science.ualberta.ca

UNIVERSITY OF
ALBERTA

Expand Your Career Opportunities

NorQuest College provides career education through diplomas and certificates in health, human services, business and industry.

NorQuest College is flexible and responsive to your needs. Through our full-time, part-time, regional and distance learning programs we will help you develop the skills you need to work effectively in any setting.

Train for an exciting career!

- Practical Nurse
- Health Care Aide
- Pharmacy Technician
- Physical Therapy Assistant
- Therapeutic Recreation
- Mental Health Rehabilitation
- Aboriginal Policing and Security
- Aboriginal Community Support Worker
- Social Work

- Business Administration
- Administrative Professional
- Hospital Unit Clerk
- Apprenticeship Prep
- Facility Service Management
- Building Service Worker
- Print Media Production
- Digital Graphics Communications
- Day Home Provider

Call: **780-644-6000** in Edmonton
Toll Free: **1-866-534-7218**
www.norquest.ca

NorQuest
COLLEGE

THE BEAR CHILDREN'S FUND

Think of it as 'Tough Love'

Since 1992, The Bear has been giving back to Edmonton's kids through The Bear Children's Fund. In the years since the Fund's inception, over $1,500,000 has been directed back into the greater Edmonton community and its charities. To make the Fund work requires the dedication of both management and staff, who have volunteered thousands of hours of their time to this worthwhile cause. As a rock station, The Bear may be loud, but it's proud too. Proud to be a part of a community as generous as Edmonton.

To apply for grants from the Bear Children's Fund please visit **www.thebearrocks.com**

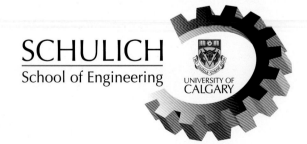

25   know, there is the tall cabinet yonder; that it was that proved him the first of Edinburgh joiners, and worthy to be their Deacon and their head: And the father's chair, and the sister's workbox, and the dear dead mother's footstool – what are they all but proofs of the Deacon's skill, and tokens of the Deacon's care for those about him?

LESLIE: I am all penitence: Forgive me this last time, and I promise you I never will again.

30   **MARY:** Candidly, now, do you think you deserve forgiveness?

LESLIE: Candidly, I do not.

MARY: Then I suppose you must have it: What have you done with Willie and my uncle?

LESLIE: I left them talking deeply: The dear old Procurator has not much thought just now for anything but those mysterious burglaries –

35   **MARY:** I know! –

LESLIE: Still, all of him that is not magistrate and official is politician and citizen; and he has been striving his hardest to undermine the Deacon's principles, and win the Deacon's vote and interest.

MARY: They are worth having, are they not?

LESLIE: The Procurator seems to think that having them makes the difference between winning and
40   losing.

MARY: Did he say so? You may rely upon it that he knows: there are not many in Edinburgh who can match with our Will.

LESLIE: There shall be as many as you please, and not one more.

MARY: How should I like to have heard you! What did uncle say? Did he speak of the Town Council
45   again? Did he tell Will what a wonderful Bailie[4] he would make? O why did you come away?

LESLIE: I could not pretend to listen any longer: The election is months off yet; and if it were not – if it were tramping upstairs this moment – drums, flags, cockades, guineas, candidates, and all! – how should I care for it? What are Whig and Tory[5] to me?

MARY: O fie on you! It is for every man to concern himself in the common weal:[6] Mr. Leslie – Leslie
50   of the Craig! – should know that much at least.

LESLIE: And be a politician like the Deacon? All in good time, but not now: I hearkened while I could, and when I could not more I slipped out and followed my heart: I hoped I should be welcome.

MARY: I suppose you mean to be unkind.

---

[4] Bailie – city official and magistrate in Scotland
[5] Whig and Tory – political parties
[6] common weal – commonwealth, the common good

LESLIE: Tit for tat: Did you not ask me why I came away? And is it unusual for a young lady to say
55   'Mr.' to the man she means to marry?

MARY: That is for the young lady to decide, sir.

LESLIE: And against that judgment there shall be no appeal?

MARY: O, if you mean to argue! –

LESLIE: I do not mean to argue: I am content to love and be loved: I think I am the happiest man in the
60   world.

MARY: That is as it should be; for I am the happiest girl.

LESLIE: Why not say the happiest wife? I have your word, and you have mine: Is not that enough?

MARY: Have you so soon forgotten? Did I not tell you how it must be as my brother wills? I can do
only as he bids me.

65   **LESLIE:** Then you have not spoken as you promised?

MARY: I have been too happy to speak.

LESLIE: I am his friend: Precious as you are, he will trust you to me: He has but to know how I love
you, Mary, and how your life is all in your love of me, to give us his blessing with a full heart.

MARY: I am sure of him: It is that which makes my happiness complete: Even to our marriage I should
70   find it hard to say 'Yes' when he said 'No.'

LESLIE: Your father is trying to speak: I'll wager he echoes you.

MARY (*to* OLD BRODIE): My poor dearie! Do you want to say anything to me? No? Is it to Mr.
Leslie, then?

LESLIE: I am listening, Mr. Brodie.

75   **MARY:** What is it, daddie?

OLD BRODIE: My son – the Deacon – Deacon Brodie – the first at school.

LESLIE: I know it, Mr. Brodie: Was I not the last in the same class? (*to* MARY.) But he seems to have
forgotten us.

MARY: O yes! His mind is well-nigh gone: He will sit for hours as you see him, and never speak nor
80   stir but at the touch of Will's hand or the sound of Will's name.

LESLIE: It is so good to sit beside you: By and by it will be always like this: You will not let me speak
to the Deacon? You are fast set upon speaking yourself? I could be so eloquent, Mary – I would touch
him: I cannot tell you how I fear to trust my happiness to anyone else – even to you!

MARY: He must hear of my good fortune from none but me: And besides, you do not understand: We
85   are not like families, we Brodies: We are so clannish, we hold so close together.

LESLIE: You Brodies, and your Deacon!

OLD BRODIE: Deacon of his craft, sir – Deacon of the Wrights – my son! If his mother – his mother – had but lived to see!

90 **MARY:** You hear how he runs on: A word about my brother and he catches it: 'Tis as if he were awake in his poor blind way to all the Deacon's care for him and all the Deacon's kindness to me: I believe he only lives in the thought of the Deacon. There, it is not so long since I was one with him: But indeed I think we are all Deacon-mad, we Brodies: Are we not, daddie dear?

BRODIE (*without, and entering*): You are a mighty magistrate, Procurator, but you seem to have met your match.

95 **SCENE II**

To these, BRODIE and LAWSON.

MARY (*curtseying*): So, uncle! you have honoured us at last.

LAWSON: *Quam primum*,[7] my dear, *quam primum*.

BRODIE: Well, father, do you know me? (*he sits beside his father and takes his hand.*)

100 **OLD BRODIE:** William – ay – Deacon: Greater man – than – his father.

BRODIE: You see, Procurator, the news is as fresh to him as it was five years ago: He was struck down before he got the Deaconship, and lives his lost life in mine.

LAWSON: Ay, I mind: He was aye ettling after a bit handle to his name:[8] He was kind of hurt when first they made me Procurator.

105 **MARY:** And what have you been talking of?

LAWSON: Just o' thae robberies, Mary: Baith[9] as a burgher and a Crown offeecial, I tak' the maist absorbing interest in thae robberies.

LESLIE: Egad, Procurator, and so do I.

BRODIE (*with a quick look at Leslie*): A dilettante[10] interest, doubtless! See what it is to be idle.

110 **LESLIE:** Faith, Brodie, I hardly know how to style it.

BRODIE: At any rate, 'tis not the interest of a victim, or we should certainly have known of it before; nor a practical tool-mongering interest, like my own; nor an interest professional and official, like the Procurator's: You can answer for that, I suppose?

---

[7] *quam primum* – as soon as possible

[8] aye ettling after a bit handle to his name – wanting a title before his name

[9] Baith – both

[10] dilettante – superficial

LESLIE: I think I can; if for no more: It's an interest of my own, you see, and is best described as
115   indescribable, and of no manner of moment to anybody: It will take no hurt if we put off its discussion till
a month of Sundays.

BRODIE: You are more fortunate than you deserve: What do you say, Procurator?

LAWSON: Ay is he! There is no a house in Edinburgh safe: The law is clean helpless, clean helpless!
A week syne it was auld Andra Simpson's in the Lawnmarket: Then, naething would set the catamarans
120   but to forgather privily wi' the Provost's ain butler, and tak' unto themselves the Provost's ain plate:[11]
And the day, information was laid before me offeecially that the limmers had made infraction, *vi et
clam*,[12] into Leddy Mar'get Dalziel's, and left her leddyship wi' no sae muckle's a spune to sup her
parritch wi': It's unbelievable, it's awful, it's anti-christian!

MARY: If you only knew them, uncle, what an example you would make! But tell me, is it not strange
125   that men should dare such things, in the midst of a city, and nothing, nothing be known of them—nothing
at all?

LESLIE: Little, indeed! But we do know that there are several in the gang, and that one at least is an
unrivalled workman.

LAWSON: Ye're right, sir; ye're vera right, Mr. Leslie: It had been deponed to me offeecially that no a
130   tradesman – no the Deacon here himsel' – could have made a cleaner job wi' Andra Simpson's shutters:
And as for the lock o' the bank – but that's an auld sang.

BRODIE: I think you believe too much, Procurator: Rumour's an ignorant jade, I tell you: I've had
occasion to see some little of their handiwork – broken cabinets, broken shutters, broken doors – and I
find them bunglers: Why, I could do it better myself!

135   **LESLIE:** Gad, Brodie, you and I might go into partnership: I back myself to watch outside, and I
suppose you could do the work of skill within?

BRODIE: An opposition company? Leslie, your mind is full of good things: Suppose we begin to-night,
and give the Procurator's house the honours of our innocence?

MARY: You could do anything, you two!

140   **LAWSON:** Onyway, Deacon, ye'd put your ill-gotten gains to a right use; they might come by the wind
but they wouldna gang wi' the water; and that's aye a *solatium*,[13] as we say: If I am to be robbit, I would
like to be robbit wi' decent folk; and no think o' my bonnie clean siller[14] dirling among jads and dicers:

---

[11] plate – silver or gold dishes
[12] *vi et clam* – with force and in secret
[13] *solatium* – compensation for emotional loss or hurt feelings
[14] siller – silver

Faith, William, the mair I think on't, the mair I'm o' Mr. Leslie's mind: Come the night, or come the morn, and I'se gie ye my free permission, and lend ye a hand in at the window forbye!

145   **BRODIE:**   Come, come, Procurator, lead not our poor clay[15] into temptation: (LESLIE *and* MARY *talk apart.*)

        LAWSON: I'm no muckle afraid for your puir clay, as ye ca't.[16]   But hark i' your ear: ye're likely, joking apart, to be gey and sune in partnership wi' Mr. Leslie: He and Mary are gey and pack, a body can see that.   Man, because my wig's pouthered do ye think I havena a green heart?   I was aince a lad mysel',

150   and I ken fine by the glint o' the e'e when a lad's fain and a lassie's willing: And, man, it's the town's talk; *communis error facit jus*,[17] ye ken.

        OLD BRODIE: Oh!

        LAWSON: See, ye're hurting your faither's hand.

        BRODIE: Dear dad, it is not good to have an ill-tempered son.

155   **LAWSON:**   What the deevil ails ye at the match?   'Od, man, he has a nice bit divot o' Fife corn-land,[18] I can tell ye, and some Bordeaux wine in his cellar!   But I needna speak o' the Bordeaux; ye'll ken the smack o't as weel's I do mysel'; onyway it's grand wine: *tantum et tale*:[19] I tell ye the *pro's*, find you the *con's*, if ye're able.

        BRODIE: You are talking in the air, as lawyers will: I prefer to drop the subject.

160   **LESLIE:**   At four o'clock to-morrow?   At my house? (*to* MARY).

        MARY: As soon as church is done. (*exit* MARY.)

        LAWSON: Ye needna be sae high and mighty, onyway.

        BRODIE: I ask your pardon, Procurator: But we Brodies—you know our failings! A bad temper and a humour of privacy.

165   **LAWSON:**   Weel, I maun be about my business: But I could tak' a doch-an-dorach,[20] William; *superflua non nocent*,[21] as we say; an extra dram hurts naebody, Mr. Leslie.

        BRODIE (*with bottle and glasses*):   Here's your old friend, Procurator: Help yourself, Leslie: Oh no, thank you, not any for me: You strong people have the advantage of me there: With my attacks, you know, I must always live a bit of a hermit's life.

---

[15] clay – weak nature

[16] ca't – call it

[17] *communis error facit jus* – what everyone is doing must be right

[18] nice bit divot o' Fife corn-land – plenty of good farmland nearby in the county of Fife

[19] *tantum et tale* – a legal term in Scottish law, meaning *take it as it stands*

[20] doch-an-dorach – a drink, a glass of whisky

[21] *superflua non nocent* – superfluous things do no harm

170 **LAWSON:** 'Od, man, that's fine; that's health o' mind and body: Mr. Leslie, here's to you, sir: 'Od, it's harder to end than to begin wi' stuff like that.

W. E. Henley and R. L. Stevenson
Henley (1849–1903) is best remembered for the
lines, *I am master of my fate: / I am captain of my soul.*
Robert Louis Stevenson (1850–94) is best remembered for his novel *Treasure Island*

38.   The **most likely** reason for the inclusion of the tableaux is that they

A.   add variety to the play

B.   show off the costumes and the detailed set

C.   are a dramatic way of presenting the situation

D.   are an ironical commentary on the audience's expectations

39.   When Mary says "You are satirical!" (line 14), the word "satirical" is

A.   correct

B.   incorrect; she should use the word *ironical*

C.   correct, but the word *sarcastic* would be better

D.   partly correct, but the word *ridiculing* would be better

40.   Leslie's tone as he speaks to Mary in the dialogue beginning in line 8 is **best** described as

A.   jeering

B.   teasing

C.   satirical

D.   mocking

41.   When Brodie says in lines 168 to 169 "With my attacks, you know," he is referring to his

A.   injuries

B.   poor health

C.   criminal behaviour

D.   disapproval of liquor

42. The detail that **best** shows Deacon Brodie's hold over his family is

    A. "'Tis a great favour, I can tell you; the place is sacred" (line 12)

    B. "and wasn't I proud to be ordered about with them!" (line 24)

    C. "Did I not tell you how it must be as my brother wills? I can only do as he bids me" (lines 63–64)

    D. "But indeed I think we are all Deacon-mad, we Brodies" (lines 91–92)

43. The detail that **best** displays the Deacon's dislike of Mary's plan to marry Leslie is

    A. "A dilettante interest, doubtless! See what it is to be idle" (line 109)

    B. "You are more fortunate than you deserve" (line 117)

    C. "See, ye're hurting your faither's hand" (line 153)

    D. "You are talking in the air, as lawyers will: I prefer to drop the subject" (line 159)

44. The procurator **most likely** uses Latin phrases because he is

    A. a pompous old fool

    B. hoping to impress the Deacon

    C. often under the influence of alcohol

    D. a magistrate and used to using Latin in court

45. Which of the following quotations contains the **best** example of dramatic irony?

    A. "You have trained me well, and I feel by him as solemnly as a true-born Brodie." (lines 15–16)

    B. "…he has been striving his hardest to undermine the Deacon's principles, and win the Deacon's vote and interest." (lines 36–37)

    C. "At any rate, 'tis not the interest of a victim, or we should certainly have known of it before; nor a practical tool-mongering interest, like my own" (lines 111–112)

    D. "Why, I could do it better myself!" (line 134)

46. Which of the following details **best** shows that the Procurator is very talkative?

A. "Baith as a burgher and a Crown offeecial, I tak' the maist absorbing interest in thae robberies" (lines 106–107)

B. "Come the night, or come the morn, and I'se gie ye my free permission, and lend ye a hand in at the window forbye" (lines 143–144)

C. "I was aince a lad mysel', and I ken fine by the glint o' the e'e when a lad's fain and a lassie's willin" (lines 149–150)

D. "But I needna speak o' the Bordeaux; ye'll ken the smack o't as weel's I do mysel'; onyway it's grand wine" (lines 156–157)

47. The tone of this extract is **best** described as

A. grim

B. comic

C. ironic

D. light-hearted

READING SIX

NOT MARBLE, NOR THE GILDED MONUMENTS

Not marble, nor the gilded monuments

Of princes, shall outlive this powerful rhyme;

But you shall shine more bright in these contents

Than unswept stone, besmeared with sluttish[1] time.

5 When wasteful war shall statues overturn,

And broils root out the work of masonry,

Nor Mars his sword nor war's quick fire shall burn

The living record of your memory.

'Gainst death and all-oblivious enmity

10 Shall you pace forth; your praise shall still find room

Even in the eyes of all posterity

That wear this world out to the ending doom.

So, till the judgement[2] that[3] yourself arise,

You live in this, and dwell in lovers' eyes.

William Shakespeare (1564–1616)

48. The **main** purpose of the rhyming couplet (lines 13–14) is to

    A. provide closure to the sonnet

    B. immortalize the speaker's love

    C. summarize the ideas in the rest of the sonnet

    D. express despair resulting from "doom" (line 12) and "judgement" (line 13)

---

[1] sluttish – slovenly, careless about dirt and mess
[2] judgement – the Day of Judgement, when in Christian, Judaic, and Muslim belief, the dead will rise and be judged
[3] that – when

49. The **best** interpretation of the phrase "and dwell in lovers' eyes" (line 14) is that the

   A.   subject of this poem will dwell wherever love is expressed between lovers

   B.   most significant quality about the speaker's love is her expressive eyes

   C.   subject of this poem will be immortalized by this poem's stating she will live in her lover's eyes

   D.   eyes of lovers will serve as a "judgement" or "standard" for other lovers

50. The theme of the immortality of art is **most strongly** represented in the quotation

   A.   "Not marble, nor the gilded monuments / Of princes, shall outlive this powerful rhyme" (lines 1–2)

   B.   "you shall shine more bright in these contents / Than unswept stone, besmeared with sluttish time" (lines 3–4)

   C.   "When wasteful war shall statues overturn, / And broils root out the work of masonry" (lines 5–6)

   D.   "'Gainst death and all-oblivious enmity / Shall you pace forth" (lines 9–10)

51. The "you" that the speaker addresses in this poem is

   A.   the poem itself

   B.   the reader of the poem

   C.   "all posterity" (line 11)

   D.   the speaker's love (line 14)

52. The **most complete** statement of this poem's controlling idea is that

    A.   love is stronger than death

    B.   deathless poetry can make someone immortal

    C.   this poem will keep the lover alive in memory until she lives again

    D.   poetry is stronger than war and death and lasts longer than brick or marble

53. This sonnet **most clearly** follows the pattern of

    A.   two quatrains containing premises (or statements) followed by a third quatrain containing a conclusion derived from the first two

    B.   one quatrain containing a statement (or thesis) followed by a second quatrain containing a contradictory statement (or antithesis) and a third quatrain containing a conclusion (or synthesis)

    C.   two groups of lines containing contradictory statements: an octave containing a statement (or argument) followed by a sextet containing an opposing statement (or contradiction)

    D.   three quatrains containing statements that express the same premise in different ways followed by a couplet sums up the rest of the poem

READING SEVEN

from WALDEN, OR, LIFE IN THE WOODS

The mass of men lead lives of quiet desperation. What is called resignation is confirmed desperation. From the desperate city you go into the desperate country, and have to console yourself with the bravery of minks and muskrats. A stereotyped but unconscious despair is concealed even under what are called the games and amusements of mankind. There is no play in them, for this comes after work. But it is a
5 characteristic of wisdom not to do desperate things.

When we consider what, to use the words of the catechism,[1] is the chief end of man, and what are the true necessaries and means of life, it appears as if men had deliberately chosen the common mode of living because they preferred it to any other. Yet they honestly think there is no choice left. But alert and healthy natures remember that the sun rose clear. It is never too late to give up our prejudices. No way of
10 thinking or doing, however ancient, can be trusted without proof. What everybody echoes or in silence passes by as true to-day may turn out to be falsehood to-morrow, mere smoke of opinion, which some had trusted for a cloud that would sprinkle fertilizing rain on their fields. What old people say you cannot do you try and find that you can. Old deeds for old people, and new deeds for new. Old people did not know enough once, perchance, to fetch fresh fuel to keep the fire a-going; new people put a little dry
15 wood under a pot, and are whirled round the globe with the speed of birds, in a way to kill old people, as the phrase is. Age is no better, hardly so well, qualified for an instructor as youth for it has not profited so much as it has lost. One may almost doubt if the wisest man has learned anything of absolute value by living. Practically, the old have no very important advice to give the young, their own experience has been so partial, and their lives have been such miserable failures, for private reasons, as they must
20 believe; and it may be that they have some faith left which belies that experience, and they are only less young than they were. I have lived some thirty years on this planet, and I have yet to hear the first syllable of valuable or even earnest advice form my seniors. They have told me nothing, and probably cannot tell me anything, to the purpose. Here is life, an experiment to a great extent untried by me; but it does not avail me that they have tried it. If I have any experience which I think valuable, I am sure to
25 reflect that this my Mentors said nothing about.

One farmer says to me, "You cannot live on vegetable food solely, for it furnishes nothing to make bones with"; and so he religiously devotes a part of his day to supplying his system with the raw material of bones; walking all the while he talks behind his oxen, which, with vegetable-made bones, jerk him and his lumbering plow along in spite of every obstacle. Some things are really necessaries of life in some

---

[1] catechism – a guide to Christian beliefs and teachings, often in the form of questions and answers

30 circles, the most helpless and diseased, which in others are luxuries merely, and in others still are entirely

unknown. The whole ground of human life seems to some to have been gone over by their predecessors,

both the heights and the valleys, and all things to have been cared for. According to Evelyn[2], "the wise

Solomon[3] prescribed ordinances for the very distances of trees; and the Roman praetors[4] have decided

how often you may go into your neighbor's land to gather the acorns which fall on it without trespass, and

35 what share belongs to that neighbour." Hippocrates[5] has even left directions how we should cut our nails;

that is, even with the ends of the fingers, neither shorter nor longer. Undoubtedly the very tedium and

ennui which presume to have exhausted the variety and joys of life are as old as Adam.

Henry David Thoreau (1817–62)
American author and philosopher; he was an advocate of
independence and simple living; he was also strongly opposed to slavery

54. According to the context of this passage, the "chief end of man" (line 6) is **best** defined as

    A. following the advice of one's community

    B. listening to the wisdom of the elderly

    C. being guided by ancient traditions

    D. making free choices

55. Instead of listening to advice from elders, the speaker recommends that people mainly

    A. listen to advice from juniors

    B. get as much experience as possible

    C. leave civilization to live closer to nature

    D. live as an example to those around themselves

---

[2] John Evelyn (1620–1706) – known for his knowledge of literature and classical history; founder of the Royal
    Society for the Advancement of Science; remembered for his diaries which gave a detailed picture of life in
    the 1600s

[3] Solomon (10th Century BC) – King of Israel; famous for his wisdom

[4] praetors – magistrates of ancient Rome; chief law officers of the state

[5] Hippocrates (460–370 BC) – Greek doctor; considered as the father of medicine; some of his teachings are still
    remembered

56. The **most notable** aspect of Thoreau's comments about the elderly is

    A.   his limited contact with the elderly

    B.   his bias against his own grandparents

    C.   the totality of his rejection of their advice

    D.   his fear of what they might have to say to him

57. The **most likely** reason for Thoreau to allude to Evelyn, Solomon, Hippocrates, and the magistrates of ancient Rome is

    A.   to quote them to support his thesis

    B.   because they were distinguished for their wisdom

    C.   as examples of the emptiness of common experience

    D.   to mention their ideas to point out the weakness of current opinion

58. The **best** description of the speaker's tone in this passage is

    A.   genial

    B.   spiteful

    C.   humorous

    D.   argumentative

READING EIGHT

This poem was written during the long-awaited visit of some friends. On the morning the friends arrived, the writer's foot was badly burned in a kitchen accident and he was unable to walk for the entire time of the visit. One day while his friends were out walking, he wrote these lines while sitting in the garden.

from THIS LIME-TREE BOWER MY PRISON

Well, they are gone, and here must I remain,

This lime-tree[1] bower[2] my prison! I have lost

Beauties and feelings, such as would have been

Most sweet to my remembrance even when age

5 Had dimm'd mine eyes to blindness! They, meanwhile,

Friends, whom I never more may meet again,

On springy heath,[3] along the hill-top edge,

Wander in gladness, and wind down, perchance,

To that still roaring dell, of which I told;

10 The roaring dell, o'erwooded, narrow, deep,

And only speckled by the mid-day sun;

Where its slim trunk the ash from rock to rock

Flings arching like a bridge; – that branchless ash,

Unsunn'd and damp, whose few poor yellow leaves

15 Ne'er tremble in the gale, yet tremble still,

Fann'd by the water-fall! And there my friends

Behold the dark green file of long lank weeds,

That all at once (a most fantastic sight!)

Still nod and drip beneath the dripping edge

20 Of the blue clay-stone.

Samuel Taylor Coleridge (1772–1834)
English poet; with William Wordsworth, he helped change the character of lyric poetry

[1] lime-tree – also called linden; a tree highly valued for its scented flowers. In July (when Coleridge's friends visited), the scent of the flowers can spread for miles.

[2] bower – shaded garden shelter

[3] heath – rough open land covered in coarse grasses and low shrubs or heather

59. The mood of the speaker is most fully represented in the lines

   A. "Well, they are gone" (line 1)

   B. "I have lost / Beauties and feelings" (lines 2–3)

   C. "Friends, whom I never more may meet again" (line 6)

   D. "wander in gladness" (line 8)

60. The exclamation mark in line 2 emphasizes the

   A. importance of the lime-tree

   B. speaker's feeling of self-pity

   C. fact that his friends have left him

   D. discomfort of any place that feels like a prison

61. The poem "This Lime-Tree Bower My Prison" is a good example of writing from the Romantic period in that it

   A. is very sober and rational

   B. is about memory and blindness

   C. derives its power from nature imagery

   D. describes a disagreement with the speaker's friends

62. The speaker of this poem is apparently speaking to

   A. no one

   B. himself

   C. the reader

   D. his absent friends

63. In lines 5 to 19, the speaker's friends

    A. see the "still roaring dell" (line 9)

    B. cross over the bridge (line 13)

    C. see "the dark green file of long lank weeds" (line 17)

    D. might have gone to the dell, but the reader cannot know for certain

64. The images found in lines 10 to 17 are **best** described as reinforcing the

    A. description of nature

    B. romantic mood of the poem

    C. author's melancholy feelings

    D. mention of old age and blindness in line 5

65. The tone of this poem is **best** described as

    A. romantic

    B. melancholy

    C. reminiscent

    D. self-pitying

ANSWERS AND SOLUTIONS – PRACTICE EXAMINATION

1.	D	12.	C	23.	B	34.	C	45.	D	56.	C
2.	D	13.	A	24.	A	35.	C	46.	D	57.	C
3.	C	14.	A	25.	C	36.	D	47.	D	58.	D
4.	A	15.	C	26.	C	37.	B	48.	C	59.	B
5.	D	16.	C	27.	C	38.	C	49.	A	60.	A
6.	A	17.	B	28.	A	39.	B	50.	A	61.	C
7.	A	18.	C	29.	B	40.	B	51.	D	62.	C
8.	A	19.	D	30.	C	41.	B	52.	C	63.	D
9.	C	20.	D	31.	D	42.	C	53.	D	64.	C
10.	C	21.	A	32.	A	43.	C	54.	D	65.	B
11.	B	22.	D	33.	D	44.	D	55.	B		

READING ONE – from *NORTHANGER ABBEY*

1. D

To some degree, all of the responses explain the narrator's "surprise" at Catherine being a heroine.

A. Her father was plain, boring, respectable, and he had never suffered any interesting difficulties. Such a father is a handicap for a heroine, but not more than a really determined young woman couldn't overcome.

B. Heroines are supposed to be good at music—it is one of the Romantic conventions of the Gothic—but this response is really only an extension of B.

C. Catherine herself could be lazy, and she was not good at arithmetic, languages, or music. These are more promising handicaps. But look at lines 52 to 73, which show the kind of learning that is really important to a heroine.

D. It is the image of a noisy, wild, grubby child rolling down a slope that really does not fit the ideal of a romantic heroine.

2. D

This is a context question. The best definition for *propensities* can be found by looking at how it is used. Lines 12 to 18 describe Catherine and they include the words *fond of*, *preferred*, *no taste for*, and *always preferring*.

These words all refer to matters of disposition, taste, or **inclination**. *Ideas*, *skills*, and *abilities* are all things learned or achieved—perhaps in spite of one's *propensities* or *inclinations*.

3. C

This question is about the supposed qualities of a heroine and requires the use of inference and interpretation.

A. Being a middle child in a large family is not heroic, but this handicap is not part of the heroine herself.

B. The narrator implies that a heroine ought to be talented at music, but there is no statement that Catherine shirked music as well as her other lessons, so this handicap does not show her at her worst.

C. This is the response that shows Catherine at her worst: shirking her lessons (that is, avoiding work).

D. A heroine can be proud and willful, but she can't have a bad heart or be bad-tempered. As far as this goes, this response is in Catherine's favour.

4. A

The narrator, of course, does not really mean that Catherine was strange and unaccountable.

A. Saying the opposite of what is meant is irony. This statement is really saying that Catherine was quite ordinary.

B. Strange and unaccountable (even when used ironically) have nothing to do with awkwardness—either physical or social. Also metaphor is a comparison in the form of a direct statement—there is no comparison in the statement.

C. Parody is a com
art (or of a gen
art: the whole
parody,[*] but t
to this brief statement.

D. The quote does show that Catherine did not have a bad character after all, but metonymy is a figure of speech that uses an attribute of something to stand for the whole. If Catherine were to be described as Miss Ordinary, then that would be metonymy.

5. D

Two of the responses fit the question; which of them is most complete?

A. It is true that much of what is said about Catherine is said in terms of what she cannot do—but none of what is said really matters.

B. Catherine has no abilities that are quite remarkable for someone so young. Her "disabilities" are to be expected in a child.

C. The story-telling is "focussed on heroic deeds in the future," but the question itself is about Catherine, not about her future.

D. None of her supposed faults is more than childish mischief, which is more or less the narrator's point.

---

[*] *Northanger Abbey* is also a satire and a love story

This question requires a prediction. What will the rest of the story be about?

A. The opening of the extract makes it clear that Catherine does become a heroine. The rest of the story must be about how that happens.

B. You have heard quite enough about how ordinary she is. Jane Austen did not become a great writer by not knowing when to stop.

C. Unless there is a plot twist that you cannot foresee, the story is about Catherine, not about her family.

D. Complete biographies belong in biographies, not in novels. A novel rarely includes details that are not part of a story.

7. **A**

Tone is the way something is said or written; tone is an indication of what a speaker or author is thinking; tone indicates attitude toward the subject and toward the audience.

A. The tone is ironic since nothing that the author said can be understood literally.

B. A Gothic tone would be characteristic of a Gothic novel. Since this is a parody, the tone cannot be Gothic.

C. Derision (the noun form of the adjective *derisive*) expresses contempt and mockery. Jane Austen's humour is not contemptuous or mocking, even though she is having a lot of fun with the conventions of the Gothic heroine.

D. Insincere means false, not genuine. Although none of the words mean what they say, the intent is not falsehood. The irony is completely sincere.

8. **A**

Today, sensible means having common sense. However, in this context, sensibility means something very different.[*] The sentence that contains sensibility has a parallel structure that could be simplified like this: *without sensibility, without real passion, without real admiration.* The three phrases are not identical, but they are about feelings. In this context, sensibility means *feelings.* The context has nothing to do with social rank, which is not mentioned until several sentences later. Admiration is only one example of sensibility.

---

[*] On an exam, be careful not to misapply word meanings that you already know. A common word can have several unusual meanings. Always pay attention to context.

9. C

This question refers to the entire reading and it requires a judgement. What is the extract about?

A. The only mention of education is in its most limited form: reciting, arithmetic for the purpose of keeping household accounts, French, music, and drawing.

B. The qualities necessary for heroism are the subject of the extract, but only in the context of being a Gothic heroine, and the author is making fun of Gothic heroines.

C. It is the absurdity of Gothic novels that is the writer's subject.

D. In the early 1800s, boys and girls received very different kinds of education (when they received any at all) but that subject is not even mentioned.

10. C

All the choices are literary genres.

A. Burlesque is the humorous treatment of serious matter through grotesque exaggeration or some other incongruity, often mocking. Burlesque does not fit. Jane Austen is often witty and always restrained; she is never grotesque or exaggerated.

B. Romantic can refer to several kinds of stories: love stories, heroic adventure, or medieval adventure. Although *Northanger Abbey* is in fact a love story, this extract does not allow that judgement.

C. Parody is a humorous imitation of another work or of a genre. This extract parodies the Gothic novel that was common in Jane Austen's day.

D. Gothic depends on certain motifs: a brooding castle (or at least a huge mansion or an ancient abbey), a heroine in distress, a brooding, mysterious hero, curses and prophecies, overwrought emotions, thunder, lightning, torrential rain, gloom, and supernatural horror. The tone of *Northanger Abbey* does not qualify it as Gothic.

READING TWO –
from PLATO'S *REPUBLIC*

11. B

The question is about limited perception. All of the quotations come from Socrates' description of the cave. However, only one makes it clear that, being unable to turn around, the prisoners can only see what is in front of them. Their perception is limited by their chains: "here they have been from their childhood, and have their legs and necks chained so that they cannot move, and can only see before them, being prevented by the chains from turning round their heads."

12. C

The liberated prisoner will be confused and uncertain (lines 34 to 36), will have to be forced out of the prison (lines 42 to 43) and will experience pain. In the end, the prisoner will congratulate himself on his release (lines 59 to 60).

A. The liberated prisoner will not regret his liberation; in the end the prisoner will be happy about being freed.

B. He will not throw caution to the wind— no, at every step progress is slow.

C. The prisoner would be so used to the imprisonment that he would have to be forced into freedom (line 43).

D. The liberated prisoner will feel pain at first, but notice the words *more intense levels*. More intense than what? More intense than the earlier levels; but there are no earlier levels of pain.

13. A

All the responses are mentioned as being likely after the prisoner's return. Which is least likely?

A. He would be least likely to be put to death, because this is mentioned only as a threat to stop him talking about what he had seen.

B. He would be unable to see as well as the others because his eyes would now be adjusted to light.

C. He would appear ridiculous because the others would have no context through which to understand his descriptions of the real world.

D. Because he could not see as well in the darkness, he would be at a disadvantage compared to those who had never left.

14. A

Notice the words *in this context*. Myths have more than one purpose, and this "myth" was invented for a particular purpose.

A. The myth does express a truth about the human condition and the limited perception that we all experience.

B. Yes, the myth does provide a vivid image that the reader can "see," but the purpose of the image is to express a truth. The image is not invented for its own sake.

C. Yes, the myth presents a thought that is too difficult for ordinary words, but what kind of thought is it? The thought is a truth about the human condition (A).

D. The moral principle is derived from the truth that has been expressed. The myth is designed to lead up to the truth, but it does not summarize the truth.

15. C

The first paragraph explains "how far our nature is enlightened or unenlightened." Each of the responses has some truth. Which is the best?

A. We are unenlightened because of the immobilizing chains, but is this the complete answer?

B. The shadows give some information, but they also deceive because they are so limited. This response not the best because "enlightened" means more than just having partial, limited knowledge.

C. "Unenlightened because of external causes beyond our control," is a better answer because the chains are only a metaphor for external causes that we do not control.

D. There is some enlightenment because of the shadows of cast by the fire, but consider that a few shadows show very little of the reality outside the cave. We are both enlightened and unenlightened.

16. C

Plato's *Republic*, from which this dialogue is taken, is largely a collection of dialogues, because Plato was recording Socrates' teaching method. These dialogues had a definite purpose.

A. They do help to simplify the story, but the story itself is not really complicated.

B. The reader is not left to infer the meaning of the argument, for Socrates himself explains what the images in the story stand for.

C. This is a technique (the Socratic method) of teaching by proceeding one step at a time through question and answer. At each stage, Glaucon (and the reader) is given a chance to respond to what has just been said.

D. One method of persuasion is to arrange for constant agreement by asking a series questions that will almost certainly be answered affirmatively (Isn't this a beautiful car? Isn't it fun to drive? I bet you'd like to own it?). Thus a final agreement is set up without the need for honest argument and clear logic. An inattentive reader could just agree along with Glaucon. However, the questions are simple and the whole argument is laid out carefully, with every step clearly explained. It seems that the purpose is instruction, not persuasion.

17. B

This question about the narrator's view of human nature requires a value judgement based on understanding of the whole extract.

A. Cynical means distrusting or contemptuous of other peoples motives. But Socrates believes that other people are unenlightened because of factors beyond their control. Even the prisoner who escapes has to be helped (forcibly) to make the first steps. The anger of the prisoners who are told about the real world is also seen as inevitable under the circumstances. So Socrates is not cynical.

B. However, Socrates seems to be realistic about human nature: there are real problems and improvement is hard.

C and D. Optimism and pessimism can describe certain philosophical viewpoints, but in ordinary speech, they simply mean having positive or negative thoughts about life. Not being given any information about the two philosophies, it is best to use the everyday meanings. Socrates is neither optimistic nor pessimistic, he simply describes the situation and says what ought to be done. He does not say how likely or unlikely he thinks the desirable outcome to be.

18. C

This question requires a judgement about degrees of unreality. The most real location is the world outside the cave, but this is not one of the responses. The best answer must be selected from among the choices given. The most real location is the one closest in some way to the real world.

A. The den (cave) is the image of unreality, so it cannot be real at all.

B. The fire casts shadows, and is itself an image of the sun. However, approaching the fire will not bring anyone closer to reality.

C. On the other side of the wall, people from the real world come and go. The objects they carry are only images, but they are more real than shadows, and they come directly from the real world. This is the most real location.

D. Shadows of images are a limited representation of images, not even a representation of reality.

19. D

The meaning of the phrase "show in a figure" must be understood by inference.

A. The shadow play is what is seen when objects are carried past the fire. These shadows are part of the story and it is the story, not just one of its parts, that is "showing in a figure."

B. A figure is like a figure of speech that contains some truth, only figure is larger—this figure is the entire story (myth). So this response is related to the answer, but is not the answer.

C. A figure is the result of calculation in arithmetic, but this meaning has nothing to do with the story.

D. This story is all about explaining a difficult truth. An illustration that demonstrates the truth describes *figure* very well.

20. D

In lines 88 to 89, Socrates is saying that anyone who wants to behave rationally should do something. All of the responses are related to this *something*.

A. Yes, we should be guided by the light of the sun, but that light is a figure that represents the light of truth.

B. Yes, we should remember that the world is a prison and that the things we see are like the prison in the story.

However, knowing we are in a prison leads to thoughts of escape or at least of the outside.

C. Yes, we should understand that nothing that we see is really true—but this is another way of saying what has been said in response B.

D. What Socrates is saying is that good is the source of truth in everything. Good is like the light of the sun by which we see the physical world. Good enlightens us in looking at the real world outside of the cave.

21. A

According to Socrates, there is a way to understand truth.

A. Socrates uses the word *inference* to describe how we come to realize that good is the author (the maker) of what is all that is beautiful and right and the source of the power to act rationally.

B. Socrates explained the truth through a figure, but not through figures of speech, which are much more limited.

C. It is very clear that studying shadows is only studying a limited part of what is real—the prisoners never see the shapes that throw the shadows.

D. The light of the sun is only a figure for the light that comes from the knowledge of good.

READING THREE – *CROSSING THE BAR*

22. D

The tone of this poem helps to establish the theme.

A. The inevitable is not directly mentioned, although it might reasonably be inferred as part of the poet's thought as he wrote the poem.

B. The silence of eternity is a commonplace phrase, a cliche, but it is not mentioned directly or indirectly in the poem. The images of silence represent peace.

C. There is no way of inferring from the poem that death is approaching the poet (except in the general sense that death is at this moment approaching all of us). This poem could be a work of keen imagination written early in life.[*]

D. The images in lines 5 to 6, 7 to 8, and 15 to 16 clearly show the acceptance of death, expressed peacefully and hopefully.

23. B

"Moaning of the bar" is a personification, a figure of speech. What does it mean? First of all, the bar is the ridge of gravel found at the shallow mouth of a harbour. Lines 5 to 6 refer to the tide, which would make a noisy rushing over the bar when rising and falling. Lines 2, 4, 8, 10, 12, 14, and 16 contain figures of speech for death. (The regularity of the numbers is probably no accident, of course. Great artists and writers do nothing by accident.)

A. Weeping is suggested by the personification in *moaning*, and the rush of water over the bar suggests weeping. This may be a secondary meaning implied in the metaphor (especially considering "sadness of farewell" in line 11).

---

[*] Tennyson was indeed fairly old when he wrote this, and we can infer that he saw death approaching, but that inference comes from other writings, not from this poem.

B. Suffering is the best answer, since "crossing the bar" is death itself (lines 4, 8, 13, 14, 16). The surface meaning (see D) is the sound of the tide over the bar, but it is immediately followed by lines 5 to 6: "But such a tide as moving seems asleep, / Too full for sound and foam." The tide is moving the ship out of the harbour of this life, across the bar, which is death, into the wide sea, which is eternity.

The poet hopes to be swept out of life on a full tide and to sweep over the death silently, "too full for sound or foam."

C. There would be shipboard sounds accompanying the leaving of harbour, but the word *moaning* disqualifies anything to do with a ship.

D. The rush of the tide over gravel is the surface meaning; however, since the poem is about death, the surface meaning is not enough.

24. A.

The poet left the exact meaning of Pilot to be inferred by the reader.

A. God is the most likely choice. Pilot is capitalized because it has special importance—this is no ordinary ship's pilot. Some other figure of great significance, an angel, or an already dead friend might also fit, but they are not in the responses.

B. Eternity is the destination. It cannot be the guide as well.

C. and D. These both refer to guides—but only at the level of the surface meaning.

25. C

An expression of attitude is closely related to tone, although tone is not asked for.

A. and B. are closely related in thought (see question 24). Both refer to a hope for a peaceful death.

C. The last expresses the hope that underlies everything in this poem. The poet refers to himself going home. The image of returning home best expresses his attitude.

D. These lines seem to be sombre, full of gloom: twilight, evening bell, and the dark. Life draws to a close, the first signs of death appear, then death itself.

26. C

Determining the reason for the three non-standard capitalizations requires a judgement of the author's intent.

A. Poetic licence refers to a non-standard usage in a poem, either for a special effect or to make the poem conform to a pattern of metre or rhyme. The three capital letters do produce an effect—but why is the poet taking poetic licence?

B. Yes, proper nouns are always capitalized, but these are not proper nouns—at least, not in the sense that is meant when quoting the rule.

C. "Time," "Place," and the "Pilot" are all very important in the poet's thought. In fact, because of that, they assume the status of proper nouns. That is why they are capitalized.

D. English did once have different rules for capitalization, but if you have read anything old enough to follow those rules, you will know that those rules are not followed in this poem. Otherwise, it is easy to see that all the other nouns are treated exactly as they are today: lower case letters for common nouns. Only three are different.

27. C

The word "that" does not have an antecedent. The poem itself makes the unexpressed antecedent clear.

A. The "I" who is embarking on a journey would be a good choice, but the word *journey* is too general. This is the last journey, the one that takes us beyond time and space. Alternative C is a more complete.

B. The tide is the image that fills the poem, but there are enough clues that the *that* is being carried by the tide. It is not the tide.

C. The soul leaving the boundary of time and space is "*that* which drew from out the boundless deep."

D. The pilot is met only after the ship leaves harbour.

28. A

Tone is an indication of what a speaker or author is thinking; tone indicates attitude toward the subject and toward the audience.

A. Calm means peaceful, quiet, without anxiety.

B. Anxious means uncertain, worried, afraid.

C. Grieving means feeling great sadness or sorrow.

D. Hopeless means without hope, despairing.

Any of these might be a normal reaction when someone faces death. Of these, *calm, peaceful, without anxiety* best describes the poet's attitude and the tone of the poem.

READING FOUR – from *THE TEMPEST*

29. B

This question must be answered by studying the printed words and lines and the scansion of the poetry.

A. When something is edited out of a text, the printers close up the space. Also, Shakespeare used so few directions that any he did use are valuable and unlikely to be discarded.

B. Look again at the lines of both the speaker and the speaker before. Counting the syllables shows that Shakespeare was indeed preserving the metre, the five feet of two syllables each, that make up iambic pentameter. The printing makes this clear to both readers and actors so the lines can be delivered properly.

C. A few lines have more or less than ten syllables to avoid monotony; otherwise, only a few lines vary in length.

D. There is sometimes a slight variation in length of line that relieves the monotony that would be produced by mechanically even lines. However, the short first line actually preserves the standard line. (See B).

30. C

Gonzalo's words have two purposes. On the one hand, he is speaking to his companions, on the other hand, he starts the scene and gives some important information.

A. The phrase contains two, possibly three, figures of speech. It is not itself an example of a figure of speech.

B. The whole play is an example of dramatic poetry.

C. Gonzalo is scene-setting. He is saying to the audience, in words that sound natural when directed to his companions, that they have been walking in circles. The audience is now filled in on what has been happening with this group of characters.

D. The words maze, forth-rights, and meanders might be considered to be metaphorical, but it is better to regard them as simple nouns. For example, a winding path may be called a meander after the winding River Meander (in Asia Minor, in what is now Turkey) or a twisted, confusing path might be called a maze, after the hedge-mazes planted as puzzles. When such a noun is used for the first time, it is a metaphor, but if such metaphors are useful, they become standard nouns and the origin is forgotten. Are these nouns examples of *dead metaphors*? It is hard to say. Alternative C remains the best answer.

31. D

Only one of the responses is connected both with hope and also with Alonso's lines spoken just before Antonio speaks.

A. No doubt Alonso is weakened by exhaustion; he says as much. However, although exhaustion may have caused his loss of hope, exhaustion has nothing to do with the fact that he had been hoping for something.

B. No doubt Alonso does feel trapped on the island, and losing hope could refer to losing hope of escape. However, there is evidence that Alonso's hope was for something else.

C. Remorse will come later, after Ariel speaks.

D. Alonso does think that his son is dead: *he is drown'd / Whom thus we stray to find.* **That is the reason he has lost hope.**

32. A

Notice that the question contains the word **examples.** A single example will not be sufficient.

A. An *allusion* is an indirect reference to something—often historical, classical, or biblical—that the writer assumes will be familiar to the audience. Unicorns and the phoenix (there is only one) are creatures of fable and legend. They are not explained, merely alluded to.

B. A *metaphor* is a comparison made as a direct statement rather than by using either of the words *like* or *as*.

C. *Metonymy* is a figure of speech that replaces the name of one thing with the name of something closely associated with it.

D. *Synecdoche* is a figure of speech similar to metonymy. Synecdoche replaces the names of something with the name of a part of that thing.

33. D

A careful reading reveals Alonso's statement of his reason for his exit. Although two of the responses give reasons that are related to Alonso's actual purpose, his own words give the correct answer.

A. Alonso does go to look for his missing son, but only in the sense that he thinks his son is drowned at the bottom of the sea and he is going to join him.

B. Because the depth and subtlety of Shakespeare's writing allows layers of interpretation, fleeing from his guilt would be a defensible answer. Alonso admits his guilt and then rushes away, intending to die. A close reading of lines 92 to 102 shows that Ariel threatens Alonso (and the others) with *lingering perdition* (slow damnation) which he can only avoid by repenting and living an honest life from now on. We might say that in admitting his guilt, but then planning suicide, Alonso shows remorse, which is often only regret at being caught out, but not repentance, which includes sorrow and the intent to do better. So in a sense Alonso is fleeing from his guilt. However, there is a simpler answer.

C. It is Antonio and Sebastian who want to fight. They respond to the exposure of their crimes with anger, not remorse. They call the spirits fiends (demons) and want to fight them.

D. Alonso does go to seek death: *my son i' the ooze is bedded, and / I'll seek him deeper than e'er plummet sounded / And with him there lie mudded.*

34. C

Ariel appearing like a harpy and making the food vanish actually suggests all the responses. Skilled writers often pack multiple meanings into images, actions, and scenes. However, one response fits the question best.

A. The shipwrecked men who have been wandering the island to the point of exhaustion are certainly hungry. That is part of the reason for the scene.

B. Naturally, a recognizable image from mythology is an allusion to mythology. The point of an illusion is to make some connection between things—in this case the action of Ariel in making the food vanish is in some ways like the actions of the harpies in a Greek myth. The point of the connection is found in alternative C.

C. **Whether or not we know the story of Jason and the Argonauts, we know that the harpies stole food from King Phineas as a punishment for a crime.**[*] **So Ariel,** *like a harpy*, **takes away the food that King Alonso is about to eat.**

---

[*] We know because the information is contained in a footnote to the reading.

D. The harpies in Greek mythology were images of horror. This fact, also known to the audience, echoes Alonso's horror when he is forced to face his crimes. Like alternatives A, B, and C, that echo is part of the reason for the scene.

35. C

Gonzalo's words to Alonso are another example of dialogue that has purposes on different levels.

A. Gonzalo certainly wants to know the reason for Alonso's strange look. Changing Alonso's mood would have to wait on learning what it is all about.

B. Alonzo is indeed on the point of confessing his crime, but Gonzalo cannot know that.

C. **The simplest and clearest answer is that only the three guilty ones see and hear Ariel. Gonzalo and the others see the food disappear and they see the spirits take away the table. They are still staring when Gonzalo notices Alonso's strange look. *In the story*, Gonzalo's words to Alonso are his natural reaction—*as part of the structure of the play*, Gonzalo's words to Alonso are Shakespeare's way of making sure that we know that Ariel was seen only by the three guilty men.**

D. Gonzalo's comment "I' the name of something holy" suggests that he is alarmed. We might suspect that he has doubts about Alonso's sanity—after all, they have only just survived a shipwreck and Alonso has just given up hope for his son. However, Gonzalo has hardly had time to think about the situation. At this point, he is simply reacting.

36. D

All the lines show some change in Alonso. Alternatives A and B show that he has given up hope of finding his son alive. Alternative C shows his loss of hope in general—since the best part of his life is past, he might as well eat the magical food; the danger doesn't matter. Alternative **D** shows that he recognizes his crimes: he has driven Prospero from Milan and he believes that he has murdered both Prospero and his infant daughter. Mourning and loss of hope are not as great a change as admitting guilt. This is made especially clear in the lines that follow the quote in alternative **D** when Alonso, convinced of his guilt and convinced that his crimes have caused the death of his son, decides to drown himself.

37. B

The word "ecstasy" has all the meanings that are given in the responses. Gonzalo's meaning is made clear by his other words and by the words and actions of the others.

A. Alonzo, moved by guilt and grief, has rushed off to throw himself into the sea (lines 124 to 125). He is moved by intense feeling. Antonio and Sebastian have rushed off, sword in hand, to fight. They are moved to intense activity, but not to intense feeling—for they will not admit their guilt. Thus this response applies only partially.

B. Rushing headlong to suicide or to fight spirits is a clear example of loss of self-control. Gonzalo sends off the younger lords to stop Alonso, Antonio, and Sebastian from harming themselves or others.

C. Feelings of remorse, guilt, and despair (Alonso) or violence (Antonio and Sebastian) are not examples of spiritual uplifting.

D. Remorse, guilt, despair, and violence are not examples of intense delight.

READING FIVE – from DEACON BRODIE, OR THE DOUBLE LIFE: A MELODRAMA IN FIVE ACTS AND EIGHT TABLEAUX

38. C

When a tableau is staged, the actors are motionless and silent. For as long as the tableau lasts, the audience simply watches.

A. There is no doubt that tableaux would add variety to a play. However, an author usually has some other purpose besides variety. In a carefully constructed play, everything has dramatic purpose.

B. The set designer would probably take the opportunity to have costumes and sets worth showing off. In some productions, such an opportunity might be reason for inserting tableaux; however, this would not be a dramatic reason—it would not likely be part of an author's intention while writing a play.

C. The titles of the tableaux presented in the whole play and the content of the first tableau show that they are a dramatic way of presenting the situation. The first tableau is the presentation of a family scene in the house of a well-to-do tradesman—and we are aware that it is one half of a double life.

D. Tableaux could be used as an ironical commentary on the audience's expectations, but there is no evidence of that in this extract. In fact, the audience knows what is going on: Brodie was infamous in his day, and the title of the play itself gives away his secret.

39. B

Satire uses some form of laughter to attack or to expose wrongdoing.

A. Leslie is not inviting laughter at Mary's wrongdoing—if her admiration is excessive, it is still not a proper object of satire.

B. **The question, "Are you sure sacred is strong enough?" means the opposite of their literal meaning. Ironic would be the accurate description. This is an example of gentle irony.**

C. Sarcasm is like irony but it is obvious, it is usually delivered in an unpleasant tone, and it is intended to hurt.

D. Satire sometimes makes use of ridicule, but the rest of Leslie's lines make it clear that he genuinely loves Mary. Ridicule is cruel and hurtful. Ridicule is not likely.

40. B

Leslie's tone as he speaks to Mary in the dialogue beginning in line 2 is **best** described as teasing.

A. *Jeering* is laughing at or shouting insults at someone in order to show lack of respect.

B. **Teasing has several meanings. One is to playfully joke with or make fun of. Leslie's words to Mary show love and affection, so when he is laughing at her excessive respect and admiration for her brother, he is teasing.**

C. Satirical has been fully answered in the solution to question 39.

D. *Mocking* means scornful laughing or jeering.

41. B

The context of Brodie's remark about his attacks is his declining to join Leslie and Lawson in a drink, saying, "Oh no, thank you, not any for me: You strong people have the advantage of me there: With my attacks, you know, I must always live a bit of a hermit's life."

A. *Attacks* might suggest *injuries*, but there is no suggestion of violence here.

B. An episode of poor health or of a health crisis is sometimes called an _attack_. Brodie also says "You strong people have the advantage of me," alluding to some weakness in himself. Thus, the best answer is poor health.

C. Since stealing was at that time punishable by death, the Deacon would have been very foolish to allude to his criminal behaviour. His earlier comment, "Why, I could do it better myself!" was different; it was a way saying that the robberies were clumsy, not the work of a master craftsman like himself.

D. Brodie may or may not disapprove of liquor. There is no evidence that he does. The fact that he has bottles and glasses ready to offer drinks to visitors suggests that he does not.

42. C

Each detail shows that Brodie has a hold over his family.

A. Sacred means holy, a strong word to use about one's brother's room. Still, Mary might be using hyperbole. She might even be laughing at herself, or joking with Leslie.

B. Here Mary is remembering her younger self, who was proud to carry out her older brother's orders. That was years ago, and her tone suggests that she is not quite the same now.

C. Mary will not marry without her brother's approval. This is the clearest example of Brodie's hold over his family. To be ready to refuse to marry the man that she loves in order to please her brother shows Brodie's strong influence over his family. [*]

D. "We are all Deacon-mad" suggests a degree of understanding. Mary is aware that her feelings are unusual.

43. C

Which detail most strongly shows Brodie's dislike?

A. and D. Brodie calls Leslie superficial and idle (line 109) as Leslie owns enough profitable land that he does not have to work with his hands, and he tells Lawson, the Procurator, that he does not want to discuss the subject of Mary and Leslie marrying. These points show his dislike, but do not show just how strong his feelings are.

---

[*] At one time, anyone under the age of 21 was a minor and could not marry without the consent of a parent or guardians. If Mary is underage, then since her mother is dead (lines 87 to 88) and her father mentally incapacitated, her brother would be her guardian. But we do not know Mary's age, so D remains the best answer.

B. This detail has nothing to do with Leslie and Mary.[*] It is about Leslie's interest in the burglaries, and it is a foreshadowing of something that will be important later in the play.

C. Brodie is so upset that he unconsciously tightens his grip on his father's hand and doesn't notice, even though he is hurting the old man. This is the strongest indication of his feelings.

44. D

We cannot be entirely sure why the procurator uses Latin phrases, but we can determine the most likely reason.

A. The procurator is old, but he seems too shrewd and humorous for pomposity (an exaggerated manner that shows self-importance).

B. Deacon Brodie has established himself as a leader in the community. He exhibits self-confidence and the habit of giving orders. It is unlikely that the procurator would think that a display of knowledge would impress such a man.

C. The procurator hints strongly at one point that he would like a drink, and he raises his glass with obvious pleasure. He also has a lot to say about Leslie's wine cellar.

---

[*] But at a glance, this detail *might* appear to mean that Brodie is telling Leslie that he is more fortunate than he deserves in winning Mary's love.

All this is evidence that he likes "to take a glass," but it is not evidence that he actually drinks too much.

D. Since he is a magistrate and at least some of his Latin is law-related, we can infer that professional habit is the reason for his using Latin.

45. D

Dramatic irony is found when the audience knows something that the characters do not, or when everyone knows something that one character does not.

A. This is Leslie's gently ironical teasing of Mary. It is not dramatic irony unless Leslie suspects Brodie, and we cannot know that from this excerpt.

B. Ironically, the Deacon has no principles. But alternative A is a far stronger example, because it comes from Deacon Brodie himself.

C. Brodie's practical tool-mongering interest is more directly practical than anyone yet realizes. Again, alternative A is a stronger example of dramatic irony, because it is a direct statement about his ability to carry out clever burglaries.

D. Do it better himself? Brodie *is* the thief. All the burglaries are his work. Since the words are from his own mouth, this is the strongest irony, and therefore the best example.

46. D

The Procurator is very talkative. What is the best example?

A. The Procurator's interest in the burglaries is sensible and natural, and he expresses no more than his interest.

B. Here the Procurator is telling a joke but he is not saying too much.

C. His words about Leslie and Mary wanting to marry are a sensible observation and possibly helpful.

D. The Procurator starts by telling Brodie that Leslie is a desirable match because he has some good land. Then he goes on at length about the Bordeaux wine in Leslie's wine cellar before remembering that he is arguing the case for Leslie and Mary marrying. This is the Procurator being talkative.

47. D

The tone of this extract is best seen in the early conversation between Leslie and Mary, and in the character of the Procurator.

A. There is nothing grim (depressing, forbidding, sternly serious) about this extract. We may infer that the rest of the play will be grimmer, but this extract is from the opening.

B. Some of the dialogue is funny, but not enough to be comic (funny enough to cause laughter).

C. The dramatic irony of the conversation about the burglary is an important element in the extract, but see D.

D. The Procurator gets some of the longest speeches, and he is intended to be a humorous character. Also the exchanges between Leslie and Mary are both loving and light-hearted— people in love do feel light-hearted.

READING SIX – NOT MARBLE, NOR THE GILDED MONUMENTS

48. C

To answer a question like this, it is necessary to understand the form of an Elizabethan (also called Shakespearean) sonnet.

A. All closing lines provide closure in some way.

B. The sonnet (and thus the couplet) is about making the memory of the poet's love deathless until the Day of Judgement at the end of the world—not forever. When she is raised from the dead, then the poet will not care about memory.

C. In all sonnets, the function of the couplet is to summarize the earlier ideas.

D. None of the imagery in this sonnet suggests despair. The word "doom" is used merely to signify the end of time, and in the final judgement, the poet's love will rise to new life.

49. A

What is the **best** interpretation of the phrase, "and dwell in lovers' eyes"?

A. The whole of line 14 states that the poet's love will live in the poem and in lovers' eyes. The two statements are intended to be similar in meaning.

B. *Lovers'* is the plural possessive. It cannot refer to the author's love herself.

C. The subject will not be immortalized by simply stating that she will be. She will be immortalized by the power of the sonnet (lines 1–4).

D. This line is plausible only because of the invented synonym for judgement. Judgement does not mean standard.

50. A

A. The immortality of art is most clearly described in the words that say that this "powerful rhyme" will outlive marble and gilded monuments.

B, C, and D all refer to the beloved, not to art

51. D

A. Although the sonnet describes its own lasting qualities, it is really about the poet's love, not about itself.

B. The poet's love is addressed as though she is the reader of the poem, but the actual reader is not addressed.

C. Posterity is only mentioned as an example of how long the poet's love will be praised.

D. The woman that the poet loves is addressed throughout the poem: "you pace forth . . . your praise . . . you live in this"

52. C

Again, the words *most complete* show that all the responses could be defended as statements of the controlling idea.

A. That love is stronger than death is an old theme, but it is not love as an abstract (but real) thing that is celebrated in this sonnet, it is the poet's love—a real woman.

B. The woman herself will not be made immortal by the poetry. Instead, her living memory will last until the Day of Judgement. After that, when the poet's love rises from the dead, we may assume that he has no further need of poetry.

C. That this poem will keep the lover alive in memory until she lives again is clearly stated in the last couplet.

D. The sonnet does claim that it is stronger than war and death and lasts longer than brick or marble—but the poem is important only as far as it preserves the living memory of the beloved.

53. D

This is one of Shakespeare's sonnets, so we can be sure it follows a sonnet form; however, there are variations within that form.

A. Shakespeare wrote sonnets of this kind, but this particular example does not contain a logical argument.

B. There are no contradictory statements in this sonnet.

C. This is a description of the form of a Petrarchian (also called Italian) sonnet.

D. All three quatrains of this sonnet express the same idea of the beloved's memory being kept alive by the power of the verse. This is one of the sonnet forms: the main idea is repeated with variations in all three quatrains, and a rhyming couplet sums up the idea.

READING SEVEN – from WALDEN, OR, LIFE IN THE WOODS

54. D

Thoreau states over and over that tradition, the community, and the old are all unreliable guides. The only guidance he values is his own, and he recommends similar free choices to his readers.

55. B

The speaker recommends that people, instead of listening to advice from elders should look for guidance somewhere else.

A. Listening to the wisdom of youth is a modern idea. It is not part of Thoreau's thought.

B. Personal experience is the only guide that Thoreau recognizes.

C. Thoreau did live close to nature, and although he recommends a simpler life, he does not talk about leaving civilization.

D. Although Thoreau is clearly giving advice, he does not speak of setting an example.

56. C

There is one very notable thing about Thoreau's comments about the elderly.

A. Since Thoreau suggests that the old have nothing valuable to pass on, one might infer limited contact with the elderly, but there is nothing in this extract to suggest that the inference is likely.

B. Thoreau's words do suggest the possibility of bias, but if such bias exists, there is no way to judge its origin from this extract.

C. Thoreau does completely reject any advice that might come from the old. The old have no very important advice to give the young, their own experience has been so partial, and their lives have been such miserable failures.

D. There is no evidence in this extract that Thoreau feared anything the elderly might say.

57. C

The advice of the old is completely rejected. Then why would Thoreau mention the famous names of long-dead people?

A. There are no quotations from the people alluded to.

B. The names alluded to were distinguished for wisdom of one kind or another, but Thoreau is not interested in that. If anything he is suggesting that the wisest did not have much to say about important matters. Hippocrates' advice on trimming fingernails seems to be sensible, but that is not what interests Thoreau. It is perhaps the most trivial of Hippocrates' teachings that has been mentioned. That is why Thoreau chose to mention it.

C. He is citing examples of the emptiness of common experience: undoubtedly, the very tedium and ennui* that presume to have exhausted the variety and the joys of life are as old as Adam.

D. The brief mention of ancient ideas is not given in contrast to current opinion. See alternative C.

58. D

Thoreau has a very distinct tone in his writing.

A. Genial means kind, good-natured, pleasant. Thoreau's tone (see line 1) is not genial.

B. Spite is petty malice. Despite some of Thoreau's comments (see line 15), the tone is not spiteful.

C. There is nothing even mildly funny about this excerpt.

D. Thoreau is writing to persuade people to agree with his point of view. He makes statements and gives examples and evidence. His tone is argumentative.

* ennui—boredom that results from lack of interest

READING EIGHT – from THIS LIME-TREE BOWER MY PRISON

59. B

All four responses show the poet's mood of melancholy and feelings of loss. Three of them refer to his absent friends, and one refers to the imagined experience of nature. The extract itself contains 20 lines, of which 6 lines contain references to the friends. The remaining 14 lines are about nature and contain clear images of trees, plants, stone, and water. There is no doubt about the poet's main interest in this extract. Thus alternative **B** is the best answer.

60. A

The best response to this question depends on information that in not stated in the poem—the reader needs some background information of the kind that is included in the introduction and footnotes.

A. A garden shelter (bower) under a tree noted for its beauty and the scent of its flowers (in July, when the poem was written) would usually be thought a very pleasant place to be.* The exclamation mark emphasizes the irony of the lime-tree bower now being a prison.

B. The poet does express feelings of self-pity (the pain of the burn may have had something to do with it), but this is not as strong a reason for the exclamation mark as is the irony.

C. "Well, they have gone, and here must I remain, / This lime-tree bower my prison!" Although the absent friends are mentioned, notice how the placement of the exclamation mark emphasizes the lime-tree bower rather than the friends.

D. Both alternatives A and D refer to prison, but alternative D is in general terms. As a rule, a specific response is better.

61. C

The answer to this question depends on knowledge of different styles of poetry.

A. The first two lines with their exclamation mark are enough to show that the poem is not meant to be sober and rational.

B. Memory and blindness lie in the future. The "beauties and feelings" that the poet has missed would be a comfort in old age—this is another example of the Romantic belief in the importance and power of nature. See alternative C.

---

* lime-tree—recall the footnote attached to the poem. This is a good example of the importance of paying attention to extra reformation that may be given by examiners.

C. During the Romantic period, natural beauty and the emotions it inspired were very important, especially to poets. The words "Beauties and feelings, such as would have been / Most sweet to my remembrance" are good examples of the Romantic attitude.

D. The poet's friends have gone for a walk; there is no mention of a disagreement.

62. C

Sometimes it is necessary to read carefully to decide who (if anyone) is being addressed in the poem.

A. The poet could be said to be addressing no one, in the sense of no one in particular. However, see alternative B. The poet is speaking to someone, even if the someone is invented for the purpose of the poem.

B. The phrase "of which I told" (line 9) shows that the poet is not speaking to himself; he is reminding someone of what he has already said.

C. The phrases "Well, they are gone" (line 1) and "of which I told" (line 9) clearly indicate that the poet is addressing someone. That someone is the reader, since he is not speaking to himself or to his friends.

D. "Well, they are gone" (line 1). If the friends were being addressed, the pronoun would have to be different: Well, you have gone.

63. D

Coleridge follows his friends in his imagination and describes what his mind's eye sees. Careful reading will show what he knows and what he supposes.

A. and C. If the friends went into the dell, then they would see the things mentioned in these responses, but we do not know for sure where they have gone.

B. A careful reading shows that there is no bridge and no word about crossing—bridge is a figure of speech. Also see alternatives A and C.

D. In the quotation "and wind down, perchance, / To that still roaring dell," the word "perchance" makes the answer clear. They *might have* gone to the dell, we cannot know for certain.

64. C

    A. and B. The lines do describe nature and reinforce the romantic mood of the poem, but both of these responses are too general.

    C. **The narrow, dark, damp, dell (narrow valley) with its branchless, almost leafless ash tree all match the author's melancholy feelings.**

    D. Lines 10 to 17 contain melancholy images, but these images *would have been / Most sweet to my remembrance* (lines 3–4). The melancholy images would have been pleasant to remember even when old and blind—melancholy feelings can be pleasant and not necessarily the result of age.

65. B

    A. The tone of the poem is romantic, but this description is too general. In what way is the tone romantic?

    B. **A pleasant melancholy when contemplating nature was a feeling valued—even indulged in—by the Romantic poets. All the thoughts and images in this poem suggest a melancholy tone.**

    C. Reminiscent (suggesting or recalling the past) does not fit: the poet is imagining the present, not remembering.

    D. There may be self-pity in the poem, but nearly all the words and images are about nature, not about the poet and his feelings.

APPENDICES

COMMON SYMBOLS

Water – fertility, life-giving, rebirth, purification and redemption

Stagnant or polluted water – corruption, evil

Fire – destruction, purification, passion, death

Earth – baseness, fertility

Air/wind – spirits, freedom, inspiration

Sun – wisdom and vision, power, life-giving, regeneration

Sunrise – birth, rebirth, joy, hope

Sunset – death

Mountains – obstacles, achievement, aspirations, awe, glory

Storms – death, evil, inner turmoil

Roads, ships, trains, railroads, etc. – journeys

Fork in the road/crossroads – choices, decisions

Doors/gates/arches – escape, opportunities, utopias, fantasy worlds, freedom

Bridges – transitions, crossing over

Walls/fences/hedges – barriers, dividing lines, prisons

Windows – freedom, longing, imprisonment

Mirrors – illusion, unreality, passage to other worlds

Birds, sky - freedom

Circle – wholeness, unity

Gardens – paradise, innocence, fertility

Desert – spiritual aridity, death, hopelessness, sterility

Lamb – innocence, Christ

Sheep – conformity

Black – evil, death, despair

White – innocence, good, redemption

Red – war, anger, blood, vengeance, love, passion

Green – growth, renewal, life, nature, envy

Yellow – sun, happiness, cowardice, betrayal

SOME COMMON LITERARY TERMS

Abstract	Abstract terms and concepts name things that are not knowable through the senses; examples are love, justice, guilt, and honour. See CONCRETE.
Allegory	A story or visual image with a second distinct meaning partially hidden. It involves a continuous parallel between two or more levels of meaning so that its persons and events correspond to their equivalents in a system of ideas or chain of events external to the story.
Alliteration	Repetition of initial consonant sounds
Allusion	Indirect or passing reference to some person, place, or event; or to a piece of literature or art. The nature of the reference is not explained because the writer relies on the reader's familiarity with it.
Analogy	A comparison that is made to explain something that is unfamiliar by presenting an example that is similar or parallel to it in some significant way
Anecdote	A brief story of an interesting incident
Antecedent Action	Action that takes place before the story opens
Antithesis	A contrast or opposition of ideas; the second part of a statement that contrasts opposite ideas
Apathy	Lack of interest
Apostrophe	A speech addressed to a dead or absent person or to an inanimate object (Do not confuse this use of apostrophe with the punctuation mark.)
Archaic	Belonging to an earlier time; words or expressions that have passed out of use are said to be archaic
Aside	Comment made by an actor and supposedly not heard by other actors
Assonance	Repetition of similar or identical vowel sounds
Ballad	A narrative poem that tells a story, often in a straightforward and dramatic manner, and often about such universals as love, honour, and courage. Ballads were once songs. Literary ballads often have the strong rhythm and the plain rhyme schemes of songs. Songs are still written in ballad form, some old ballads are still sung, and some literary ballads have been set to music. Samuel Taylor Coleridge's "The Rime of the Ancient Mariner" is an example of a literary ballad.
Blank Verse	Poetry written in unrhymed iambic pentameters
Caricature	A distorted representation to produce a comic or ridiculous effect
Chronological	In order of time
Cliché	An overused expression; one that has become stale through overuse
Colloquial	Informal, suitable for everyday speech but not for formal writing
Concrete	A concrete thing exists in a solid, physical; and is knowable through the senses; trees, copper, and kangaroos are all examples of concrete things. See ABSTRACT.
Connotation	Implied or additional meaning that a word or phrase imparts. Such meaning is often subjective. See also DENOTATION.
Deduction	A conclusion reached by logic or reasoning, or by examining all the available information
Denotation	The explicit or direct meaning of a word or expression, aside from the impressions it creates. These are the meanings listed in dictionaries. See also CONNOTATION.
Discrepancy	Distinct difference between two things that should not be different, or that should correspond
Dissonance	Harsh sound or discordance; in poetry, a harsh jarring combination of sounds

Epic	A long poem that is often about a heroic character. The style is elevated and the poetry often represents religious or cultural ideals; the *Iliad* and the *Odyssey* are examples of epics
Epilogue	A final address to the audience, often delivered by a character in a drama
Fantasy	A literary genre; generally contains events, characters, or settings that would not be possible in real life
Foreshadowing	A storytelling technique; something early in the story hints at later events
Free Verse	Is usually written in variable rhythmic cadences; it may be rhymed or unrhymed, but the rhymes are likely to be irregular and may not occur at the end of lines
Hyperbole	A figure of speech that uses exaggeration for effect
Imagery	Language that evokes sensory impressions
Imitative Harmony	Words that seem to imitate the sounds to which they refer; *buzz* and *whisper* are examples of imitative harmony; also called ONOMATOPOEIA.
Interior Monologue	Conversation-like thoughts of a character
Irony	The difference—in actions or words—between reality and appearance. Authors use irony for both serious and humorous effects. Irony can also be a technique for indicating, through character or plot development, the writer's own attitude toward some element of the story.
Jargon	Special vocabulary of a particular group or activity; sometimes used to refer to confusing or unintelligible language
Justification	The giving of reasons or support; for example, giving an argument or reason that shows that an action or belief is reasonable or true
Juxtaposition (or contrast)	The deliberate contrast of characters, settings, or situations for effect; the effect may be a demonstration of character or heightening of mood
Lyric	A poem that expresses the private emotions or thoughts of the writer; sonnets, odes, and elegies are examples of lyrics
Metamorphosis	An alteration in appearance or character
Metaphor	Comparison without using the words *like* or *as*
Metrical poetry	Is written in regular, repeating rhythms and may be rhymed or unrhymed; when rhymes are used, they are generally regular, like the rhythm, and are often found at the end of the line
Monologue	A literary form; an oral or written composition in which only one person speaks
Mood	In a story, the atmosphere; when a writer orders the setting, action, and characters of a story so as to suggest a dominant emotion or patterns of emotions, this emotional pattern is the mood of the story. Also a person's state of mind or complex of emotions at any given time.
Motif	A recurring theme, situation, incident, idea, image, or character type that is found in literature
Ode	A poem expressing lofty emotion; odes often celebrate an event or are addressed to nature or to some admired person, place, or thing; an example is "Ode to a Grecian Urn" by John Keats
Onomatopoeia	Words that seem to imitate the sounds to which they refer.
Oxymoron	A combination of two usually contradictory terms in a compressed paradox; for example, "the living dead." An oxymoron is like a metaphor in that it expresses in words some truth that cannot be understood literally; *truthful lies* is an oxymoron that describes metaphors
Parable	A short, often simple story that teaches or explains a lesson—often a moral or religious lesson

Paradox	An apparently self-contradictory statement that is, in fact, true
Parallelism	The arrangement of similarly constructed clauses, verses, or sentences
Parenthetical	A word, phrase, or passage (sometimes within parentheses) that explains or modifies a thought
Personification	The giving of human attributes to objects or to abstract ideas
Prologue	An introduction to a play, often delivered by the chorus (in ancient Greece, a group, but in modern plays, one actor) who plays no part in the following action
Pun	A humorous expression that depends on a double meaning, either between different senses of the same word or between two similar sounding words
Rhetoric	The art of speaking or writing
Rhetorical Question	A question for which a reply is not required or even wanted; the question is asked for effect. Often, a rhetorical question is a way of making a statement: *Is there anyone who does not believe in freedom?* really means *Everyone believes in freedom.*
Ridicule	Contemptuous laughter or derision (contempt and mockery); ridicule may be an element of satire
Satire	A form of writing that exposes the failings of individuals, institutions, or societies to ridicule or scorn in order to correct or expose some evil or wrongdoing
Simile	Comparison using the words *like* or *as*
Soliloquy	A speech by a character who is alone on stage, or whose presence is unrecognized by the other characters; the purpose is to make the audience aware of the character's thoughts or to give information concerning other characters or about the action
Sonnet	A lyric poem fourteen lines long and usually written in iambic pentameter. The Shakespearean sonnet consists of three quatrains (four-line stanzas) and a couplet (two lines), all written to a strict end-rhyme scheme (abab cdcd efef gg). The development of the poet's thoughts is also structured. There are several methods: one method is to use each quatrain for different points in an argument and the couplet for the resolution of the argument. Because of the complexity of the sonnet, poets sometimes find it a suitable form for expressing the complexity of thought and emotion.
Symbol	Anything that stands for or represents something other than itself. In literature, a symbol is a word or phrase referring to an object, scene, or action that also has some further significance associated with it. For example, a rose is a common symbol of love. Many symbols, such as flags, are universally recognized. Other symbols are not so universally defined. They do not acquire a meaning until they are defined by how they are used in a story. They may even suggest more than one meaning. For example, snow might be used to symbolize goodness because of its cleanness, or cruelty because of its coldness. Symbols are often contained in story titles; in character and place names; in classical, literary, and historical allusions and references; in images or figures that appear at important points in a story; and in images that either receive special emphasis or are repeated.
Thesis	A statement that is made as the first step in an argument or a demonstration
Tone	A particular way of speaking or writing. Tone may also describe the general feeling of a piece of work. It can demonstrate the writer's attitude toward characters, settings, conflicts, and so forth. The many kinds of tone include thoughtful, chatty, formal, tragic, or silly; tone can also be a complex mixture of attitudes. Different tones can cause readers to experience such varying emotions as pity, fear, horror, or humour.

DIRECTING WORDS

The following list of directory words and definitions may help you plan your writing. For example, a particular discussion might include assessment, description, illustrations, or an outline of how an extended argument could be developed.

DIRECTING WORD	DEFINITION
Agree Or Disagree	Support or contradict a statement; give the positive or negative features; express an informed opinion one way or the other; list the advantages for or against
Assess	Estimate the value of something based on some criteria; present an informed judgement. The word "assess" strongly suggests that two schools of thought exist about a given subject. Assessing usually involves weighing the relative merit of conflicting points of view; e.g., negative vs. positive, strong vs. weak components, long-range vs. short-term
Compare	Point out similarities or differences; describe the relationship between two things; often used in conjunction with CONTRAST
Contrast	Show or emphasize differences when compared; see COMPARE
Describe	Give a detailed or graphic account of an object, event, or sequence of events
Discuss	Present the various points of view in a debate or argument; write at length about a given subject; engage in written discourse on a particular topic
Explain	Give an account of what the essence of something is, how something works, or why something is the way it is; may be accomplished by paraphrasing, providing reasons or examples, or by giving a step-by-step account
Identify	Establish the identity of something; establish the unique qualities of something; provide the name of something
Illustrate	Give concrete examples to clarify; provide explanatory or decorative features
List	Itemize names, ideas, or things that belong to a particular class or group
Outline	Give a written description of only the main features; summarize the principal parts of a thing, an idea, or an event
Show (that)	Give facts, reasons, illustrations or examples, to support an idea or proposition
State	Give the key points; declare
Suggest	Propose alternatives, options, or solutions
Support	Defend or agree with a particular point of view; give evidence, reasons, or examples
Trace	Outline the development of something; describe a specified sequence

SOME EASILY CONFUSED WORDS

• a, an	• Both are articles. Use *a* before a consonant **sound**, *an* before a vowel **sound**	• a box, a unicorn, a hit • an apple, an historian, an heir
• accept • except	• receive, agree to • exclude	• I accept your explanation. • Everyone except you may go.
• adapt • adopt	• change to suit the circumstances • make one's own	• Adapt your reading style to the nature of the reading that is assigned. • You had better adopt a new method.
• adverse • averse	• unfavourable • opposed to, reluctant to do	• The adverse road conditions made travel impossible. • Many of us are averse to homework.
• advice • advise	• helpful suggestions • offer advice	• Will you give us your advice? • No, I cannot advise you.
• affect • effect	• influence • result	• A blow to the head can affect memory. • One effect of a blow to the head is memory loss.
• affect • affective	• influence • related to the emotions	• A blow to the head can affect memory. • Depression is a serious affective illness.
• aggravate • irritate, annoy	• make worse • bother, harass, make impatient or angry	• Loss of sleep aggravated his illness. • Your silly laugh is irritating. Are you trying to annoy us?
• all ready • already	• completely prepared • an adverb meaning *before now*	• She is all ready for the trip. • Three of us have already left.
• all together • altogether	• everyone is present • an adverb meaning *completely*	• We are all together in this picture. • Well! I was altogether confused.
• allude • elude	• refer to something (see allusion) • avoid, slip away from	• He alluded to Shakespeare's verse. • The fox eluded the hounds.
• allusion • reference • quotation	• indirect mention • clear, direct mention • repetition of exact spoken or written words	• He made an allusion to his mysterious journey. • He referred to page one, paragraph 3. • He quoted the first lines of his orders.
• allusion • illusion	• indirect mention • idea or image that is not what it appears	• He made an allusion to his mysterious journey. • The ghost was an illusion produced by the moonlight.
• among • between	• usually used of several • usually used of two	• The inheritance was divided among the five sisters. • The inheritance was divided between Manfred and Louisa.
• ante • anti	• before • against	• Antebellum refers to the period before the American Civil War. • He made an anti-war speech.
• anxious • eager	• worried • enthusiastic and impatient	• He is anxious about his marks. • He is eager to hear his results.
• anyone • any one	• an indefinite pronoun • a noun phrase similar in meaning to the pronoun *anyone*; it emphasizes the number; *any* is an adjective, *one* is a pronoun	• Anyone may answer the question. • Any one of your poems may be submitted.
• avoid • avert	• stay away from • prevent	• He wishes to avoid trouble. • We may be able to avert war by preparing for it.
• awhile • a while	• a brief time; do not use with *for* • a period of time; used with for	• We sat awhile and rested. • I shall be gone for a while.
• bad • badly	• an adjective • an adverb	• I feel bad about that. • He behaved badly.
• beside • besides	• by the side of • in addition to	• The spoon is beside the cup. • Besides, it makes a good joke.

• bring • take	• bring here • take there	• Bring your friend when you come to visit. • Take your coat with you when you go.
• can • may	• is able to • has permission to	• You can go wherever you want. • You may not ignore the traffic laws.
• capital • capitol	• main, most important • a building for lawmakers to meet	• Victoria is a capital city. • The Capitol houses the US Congress.
• climatic • climactic	• refers to climate • highest moment	• Vancouver has a mild climate. • At the climactic moment in the play, the fire alarm went off.
• complement • compliment	• something that completes something else • praise	• Our ship now has a full complement of sailors. Your essay complements the original play. • We complimented the conductor.
• conscience • conscious	• awareness of right and wrong • awake and aware	• The thief's conscience began to trouble him. • When you are awake, you are conscious.
• censor • censure	• prohibit from publication • condemn	• Despite lip service to free speech, unpopular views are frequently censored. • The principal censured their unprincipled actions.
• continual • continuous	• happening over and over • uninterrupted, without stopping	• In this town, rain falls continually. • The rain fell continuously for five days.
• council • councilor	• group of administrators or advisors • a council member	• The council will meet to decide. • All the councilors must be present.
• counsel • counselor	• advice • an advisor	• I counseled him to stay in school. • I also advised him to see the school counselor.
• disinterested • uninterested	• not favouring one side or another, without bias • not interested	• We expect judges to be disinterested. • She is uninterested interested in origami.
• duel • dual	• a formal conflict • double	• The two enraged courtiers fought a duel. • This car has a dual exhaust.
• effect • effective	• cause a change • capable of producing a result	• Yes, I think we can effect improvements. • That is an effective method of effecting change.
• elicit • illicit	• call forth, bring out, obtain • illegal	• With great skill, the lawyer elicited a truthful response. • We fear he has been dealing in illicit drugs.
• eminent • imminent	• distinguished, famous • about to happen	• An eminent professor lectured on wave dynamics. • Disaster is imminent. Take immediate precautions.
• ensure • insure	• make sure something will happen • take precautions in case something happens	• Please ensure that enough supplies are stockpiled. • We will insure against disaster by being prepared.
• every one • everyone	• noun phrase • pronoun	• Every one of the books is waterlogged. • Everyone please listen.
• every day • everyday	• noun phrase • adjective	• We work hard every day. • He wore his everyday clothes to the party.
• explicit • implicit	• clear, detailed • not stated, but understood	• Even though they were given explicit instructions, they still got it wrong. • Their distaste for the job was implicit in their actions.
• farther • further	• often used for used for distance • additional	• Go one mile farther. • Take further steps.
• few • little	• use with things that can be numbered • use with things that cannot be numbered	• We saw few cars on our way. • Even so, he took little care with his work.
• fewer • less	• as above • as above	• Our goal is to have fewer cars on the road. • Our goal is less pollution.

• good • well	• an adjective • an adverb	• He always did good work. • He always worked well.
• imply • impute • infer	• suggest • to attribute something (often negatively) to someone • come to a conclusion	• Are you implying that I am lying? • He imputes dishonesty to every politician. • I infer that this experiment has been successful.
• ingenious • ingenuous	• clever and skilful • foolishly simple and trusting	• That is an ingenious invention. • She is ingenuous enough to still trust him.
• lay • lie	• transitive verb: I, you, we, they lay (laid, have laid) a parcel on a table; he, she, it lays (laid, has laid) a parcel on the shelf • intransitive verb: I, you, we, they lie (lay, have lain) down to sleep; he, she, it lies (lay, has lain) down to sleep	• Just lay that parcel over there on the counter. • When we reached the peak, we collapsed on the ground and lie still.
• learn • teach	• acquire knowledge • give knowledge	• I can learn that quickly. • We learn best when we teach.
• literally • figuratively	• exact, precise, the true meaning; without exaggeration • not exact and factual; used to suggest similarities	• I have literally no money: my pockets are empty. • When I said that I wouldn't take a million dollars for that horse, I spoke figuratively. Of course we can agree on a price.
• loose • lose	• not tight • fail to keep, not have, be defeated	• I have a loose tooth. • Even though we lost the fight, let's not lose our sense of humour.
• media • medium	• media is the plural • medium is the singular	• Television, newspapers, and radio are examples of communications media. • Television is one medium of communication.
• nauseated • nauseous	• feeling sick • sickening	• That smell makes me feel nauseated. I'm afraid I might be sick. • That smell is nauseous.
• number • amount	• use with things that can be counted (a large number of people) • use with things that cannot be counted (a large amount of waste)	• I'll take a number of those books. • We have a large amount of grain stockpiled for emergencies.
• phenomenon • phenomena • phenomenal	• a remarkable thing or event • plural of phenomenon • amazing	• That young singer is an absolute phenomenon. • Yes, we've had quite a few phenomena like her lately. • That was a phenomenal series of home runs.
• precede • proceed	• come before • go ahead	• Youth precedes old age. • Let us proceed to the next point.
• prescribe • proscribe	• command • forbid	• I prescribe exercise and fresh air. • Performance enhancing drugs are absolutely proscribed.
• principal • principle	• most important • basic belief or standard	• The principal part is this one. • I can not yield on this point. It is a matter of principle.
• quote • quotation	• verb • noun	• Let me quote her exact words. • A quotation consisting of six lines of Shakespeare opened the play.
• raise • rise	• transitive verb • intransitive verb	• Raise your hand. • The sun rises in the morning.
• real • really	• adjective • adverb	• That is a real jewel. • You really have worked hard.

• rebut • refute	• dispute, disagree, make an answer • disprove	• To rebut is to make an argument against something, but not necessarily successfully. • If something is refuted, then it is shown to be false.
• set • sit	• place • rest upon	• Set the chair in the corner. • Sit on this chair over here.
• since • because	• a preposition used in an adverbial phrase showing time; or a subordinate conjunction • a subordinate conjunction	• Since yesterday, she has been working. • Since you are late, you must sign in. • Because you are late, you must sign in.
• that • which	• *that* introduces a restrictive clause, an essential part of the idea in the sentence • *which* introduces a non-restrictive clause, a non-essential part that could be removed from the sentence	• Here are the reports that you ordered. • My new book, which I promised to give to you, is missing.
• their • they're • there • there're	• possessive pronoun • contraction of *they are* • adverb, pronoun, interjection • non-standard contraction imitating speech	• Their car is smashed. • They're feeling bad about it. • We'll go there. There are three muffins left. There! Now you've done it! • There're four days left.
• to • too • two	• preposition • adverb • number	• Let's go to town. • You are too harsh. I want that one, too. • Two dogs barked.
• tortuous • torturous	• winding, twisted • like torture	• The lawyer's tortuous arguments confused everyone. • Twelve hours of torturous effort followed.
• unique • unusual	• one of a kind (never add a modifier to unique) • not common	• The Cullinan diamond is unique. • Any very large diamond is unusual.
• whose • who's	• interrogative pronoun • contraction of *who is*	• Whose diamond is this? • Who's this strange man?
• your • you're	• possessive pronoun • contraction of you are	• Your Rolls Royce has arrived. • No doubt you're glad to see it.

EXAMPLES OF CONJUNCTIVE ADVERBS

Adverbs like these can be used with a semicolon to join independent clauses into compound sentences.

For example:

We have presented our case completely; on the other hand, there is no telling how the judge will respond.

I like your pitch; however, it sounds too much like an Indiana Jones *movie.*

Here are some common conjunctive adverbs.

accordingly	incidentally	on the contrary
as a result	indeed	on the other hand
at the same time	instead	otherwise
consequently	likewise	similarly
finally	meanwhile	so far
for example	moreover	still
for instance	namely	thereafter
furthermore	nevertheless	therefore
hence	next	thus
however	nonetheless	undoubtedly
in fact	of course	

EXAMPLES OF SUBORDINATING CONJUNCTIONS

Subordinating conjunctions introduce a subordinate clause. For example:
After the party, we will need to lock the hall.
Unless you go, the party will be a bore.

Here are some of the more common subordinating conjunctions.

after	before	that	when
although	even though	though	where
as	if	unless	whether
as if	than	until	while
because			

USEFUL LINKING VERBS

A linking verb can be used in either of two sentence patterns:
noun + linking verb + adjective
My new car is black.
She turned green.
Our well ran dry.
noun + linking verb + noun
My aunt is the ombudsman.
Nevertheless, they remain fools.
Our efforts proved futile.

Linking Verbs Expressing a *State of Being*	Linking Verbs Expressing a *Change in State*
taste	turn
appear	become
be	get
feel	grow
lay	fall
look	prove
remain	run
seem	
smelled	
sound	
stay	

COMMONLY USED IRREGULAR VERBS[1]

Most lists of irregular verbs are arranged in alphabetical order. Although that order has its uses, it does make the irregular verbs appear to be a random collection of variations. Because the following lists of irregular verbs have been sorted to show the patterns of variation, they can be more easily used for review and study. For example, the first list illustrates how many verbs do not change.

- **Many people who speak English as their mother tongue do not know all the common English irregular verbs. Use these lists to check your knowledge.**

1	Base Verb	Simple Past	Past Participle	1	Base Verb	Simple Past	Past Participle
	burst	burst	burst		let	let	let
	cast	cast	cast		put	put	put
	cost	cost	cost		quit	quit	quit
	cut	cut	cut		read	read	read
	fit	fit	fit		set	set	set
	hit	hit	hit		shut	shut	shut
	hurt	hurt	hurt		spread	spread	spread

2	Base Verb	Simple Past	Past Participle	2	Base Verb	Simple Past	Past Participle
	bend	bent	bent		make	made	made
	bind	bound	bound		mean	meant	meant
	bring	brought	brought		meet	met	met
	build	built	built		pay	paid	paid
	buy	bought	bought		say	said	said
	catch	caught	caught		seek	sought	sought
	deal	dealt	dealt		sell	sold	sold
	dive	dived	dived		send	sent	sent
	feed	fed	fed		shine	shone	shone
	feel	felt	felt		shoot	shot	shot
	fight	fought	fought		sit	sat	sat
	find	found	found		sleep	slept	slept
	hang	hung	hung		spend	spent	spent
	hang[2]	hanged	hanged		stand	stood	stood
	hold	held	held		stick	stuck	stuck
	have	had	had		strike	struck	struck
	hear	heard	heard		sweep	swept	swept
	keep	kept	kept		swing	swung	swung
	lay	laid	laid		teach	taught	taught
	lead	led	led		tell	told	told
	leave	left	left		think	thought	thought
	lend	lent	lent		understand	understood	understood
	light	lit	lit		win	won	won
	lose	lost	lost				

---

[1] There are variations, some literary, some in common use. There are also Americanisms, such as *dove* used as the past tense of *dive*. However, students may confidently use the verb forms in these lists.

[2] Hang, hanged, hanged—this verb is used only when referring to execution by hanging.

3	Base Verb	Simple Past	Past Participle
	begin	began	begun
	drink	drank	drunk
	ring	rang	rung
	sing	sang	sung
	sink	sank	sunk
	spring	sprang	sprung
	swim	swam	swum

4	Base Verb	Simple Past	Past Participle
	arise	arose	arisen
	drive	drove	driven
	ride	rode	ridden
	rise	rose	risen
	write	wrote	written

5	Base Verb	Simple Past	Past Participle
	break	broke	broken
	choose	chose	chosen
	speak	spoke	spoken
	steal	stole	stolen
	wake	woke	woken

6	Base Verb	Simple Past	Past Participle
	fall	fell	fallen
	see	saw	seen
	shake	shook	shaken
	take	took	taken
	undertake	undertook	undertaken

7	Base Verb	Simple Past	Past Participle
	become	became	become
	come	came	come
	overcome	overcame	overcome
	run	ran	run

8	Base Verb	Simple Past	Past Participle
	eat	ate	eaten
	forbid	forbade	forbidden
	forget	forgot	forgotten
	forgive	forgave	forgiven
	freeze	froze	frozen
	get	got	gotten (got)
	give	gave	given
	hide	hid	hidden

9	Base Verb	Simple Past	Past Participle
	bear	bore	borne
	beat	beat	beaten
	blow	blew	blown
	do	did	done
	draw	drew	drawn
	fly	flew	flown
	grow	grew	grown
	know	knew	known
	tear	tore	torn
	throw	threw	thrown
	wear	wore	worn
	withdraw	withdrew	withdrawn

10	Base Verb	Simple Past	Past Participle
	be	was (were)	been
	go	went	gone
	lie	lay	lain
	show	showed	shown
	slay	slew	slain

KINDS OF PRONOUNS

You should be able to recognize the different kinds of pronouns.

Kinds of Pronouns	Examples	Example Sentences
Demonstrative	this, that, these, those	I want to enter *this* in the exhibition.
Interrogative	who, whom, which, what, whoever, whomever, whichever, whatever	*Who* said that?
Relative	who, whom, that, which, whoever, whomever, whichever	Choose *whichever* you like.
Indefinite	all, another, any, anybody, anyone, anything, each, everybody, everyone, everything, few, many, nobody, none, one, several, some, somebody, someone	*Many* have asked that question.
Reflexive	myself, yourself, herself, himself, itself, ourselves, yourselves, themselves	She did the job *herself*. He wanted the land for *himself*.
Intensive	myself, yourself, herself, himself, itself, ourselves, yourselves, themselves	The professor *himself* was not sure of the answer.

Notice the **reflexive** pronouns. These are often used incorrectly. The examples in the chart show the correct uses of the reflexive pronoun. When the reflexive is used immediately after the noun then it is an **intensifier**.

EDITING SYNTAX, GRAMMAR, AND USAGE

You study grammar to understand the structure and operation of language, so that you can use words more easily, and communicate more clearly. Understanding the grammar—the names of the parts of speech, kinds of sentences, rules for the agreement of parts of sentences—gives you a common vocabulary so that you can speak about language. If an editor says to an author, "Use the *objective case* of that pronoun," then it is helpful for the author to know what the objective case is. If the Diploma Examiners give advice about using varied syntax and different kinds of sentences, it is desirable to know what they are talking about—and what they will want to see when they are marking.

1. GRAMMAR

A. SENTENCES

> Every **sentence** contains at least a noun and a verb; that is, a sentence must have a **subject** and a **predicate**. A sentence is a group of words that expresses a complete thought, begins with a capital letter, and ends with a period or other punctuation. Even a sentence fragment, which is a sentence error, follows the last two rules.

Parts of speech are the building blocks of sentences.

The **subject** is a noun and everything attached to that noun	The **predicate** is a verb and everything attached to that verb
Cattle	graze.
A tall *girl*	*ran* to the gate.
Penelope, the faithful wife of Odysseus,	slowly *wove* an intricate tapestry.

Sometimes a complete sentence seems to be missing a necessary part. *Stop!* is an example, since it seems to have no subject. However, the subject, *you*, is understood.[*] Similarly, some sentences contain parts of speech that are understood and omitted.

- Here is a copy of the assignment I gave you. (*that I gave to you*)
- Write me when you find work. (*Write to me*)

> As a general rule, do not write sentence fragments (incomplete sentences). When you edit, look for fragments and rewrite them into complete sentences.

---

[*] Such sentences are called minor sentences. They are not fragments and are acceptable.

Of course, unless you simply forgot to write something down, you are not likely to use a fragment like this:

- While watching television.

However, you might lose track of a more complicated sentence:

- While watching television and keeping one eye on the clock, Emma began to wonder if, despite what she had been told and in spite of what she had promised, that she was already late.

Something has happened here. The sentence needs rewriting.

2.   GRAMMAR AND THE SENTENCE

Of the eight **parts of speech** that combine to make sentences, at least two are required to make a sentence: a noun—the **subject**—and a verb—the **predicate**. Of course, subjects and predicates are usually more complicated than this.

One important point to remember is that **phrases** (groups of words that belong together) always function as parts of speech when they are used in a sentence. Also, a **clause** is a group of words that contains a subject and a predicate—but a clause is not always a sentence.

Here is a review of the parts of speech and some of the important applications for writing sentences.

A.   NOUNS

Nouns name **things**: soil, tree, liberty, unicorn, country, William Shakespeare.

Nominals are words or phrases that act like nouns:

- That *red* is the one I want.
- Choosing the right word can be hard.

Appositives are words and phrases that rename a noun.

- Abigail Moriarty, *the notorious swindler*, is back in town.
- Jane, the friend I told you about, is going to visit.

An appositive must have the same grammatical relationship to the other parts of the sentence as the noun it renames. In other words, if you were to cross out the original nouns and the extra commas, then you would still have a perfectly complete sentence.

- The notorious swindler is back in town.

> From these examples, you see that appositives are also nominals. Remember that a word or group of words can act as more than one part of speech. It all depends on how the word is used.

Nouns can be made by simply adding *–ing* to a verb. The result is **gerund**, or a verb functioning as a noun.

- *Swimming* is a healthy exercise.
- Healthy exercise includes *swimming*.

Similarly, an **infinitive**, a verb in its infinitive form (the base verb plus *to*), can be a noun:

- *To swim* is healthy.
- Her goal is to become a veterinarian.

When reading or hearing an unfamiliar word, or working with words, it might be helpful to remember that some nouns have distinctive endings; here are some of them:

-ment (resentment, government, parliament)

-ism (communism, liberalism)

-ness (happiness, wellness)

-tion (multiplication, domestication)

-ty (equality, fraternity)

-ence or **–ance** (independence, indifference, temperance, deliverance)

In writing, a typical noun ending can be used to turn a word into a special noun for particular effect. For example, someone who is tired of receiving phone calls might say, "This *telephonation* is driving me crazy!"

> This information about different forms of nouns suggests an important point. Try to think about language: think about *how words are used* and think about *how words could be used.*

B. VERBS

Verbs describe **actions** (jump, scratch, study, think, laugh) or **states of being** (is, are, was, exist, seem, belong).

The important thing to remember is that many verbs are transitive: that is, they take objects. When a verb *takes an object*, the action of the verb is transferred directly or indirectly to something.

Direct object:

- Casey hit the *ball*.

Indirect object:

- Miss Jones handed a paper to *Gretchen*.
- Miss Jones handed *Gretchen* a paper.

The last two examples also have a direct object, *paper*.

Linking verbs describe states of being.

- most often forms of the verb *to be*
- also verbs like *appear, seem*
- also the five sense verbs: look, sound, smell, feel, taste
- also verbs that indicate changes in states of being, such as *turn, become, go*
- Linking verbs connect subjects and their compliments. The two kinds of **compliments** supply more information about the subject:

i)   **Noun complements**

- Their uncle is a *lawyer.*
- He became a *lawyer.*

The noun compliment is sometimes called the **predicate nominative**, or **subjective complement**.

ii)   **Adjective complements**

- Cassandra was *ill.* She became *ill* quite suddenly.
- Sally turned *red.*
- I feel *sick.*
- The milk turned *sour.*

Most verbs in English are regular and cause little trouble. Consider the verb *to jump* as a reminder of how simple the pattern is:

Persons	Present tense	Present participle	Past tense	Past participle
I	jump	jump	jumped	have jumped
you				
he, she, it	jumps			
we	jump			
you				
they				

Notice the one exception to the pattern: the third person singular requires an –s ending. Remember that all verbs follow the same pattern: the third person singular requires an –s ending. All the other tenses – *will jump, will have jumped, should have been jumping, will have been jumping* – are made up from the basic forms and the auxiliary verbs *be* and *have.*

Nearly all verbs in the English language are regular.

Unfortunately, some verbs—about 300 of them, although not all are common—are not regular, and that is a problem for some students. The irregular verbs—for example, *bring, brought, have brought*; and *go, went, have gone*—must be properly used. However, while errors in the use of irregular verbs mar speech and writing, the irregular English verbs are beyond the scope of this study guide. If you have any doubt about your ability to use these verbs properly, consider obtaining an English language handbook or examining some of the English as a Second Language sites available on the Internet.

Usage Notes

When writing, do not forget to check that all your subjects and verbs agree in number and tense. Agreement can be confusing if you only look at the noun nearest the verb.

Incorrect:	The delicate carrots so carefully and skilfully baked into this delicious vegetable pie *is* steaming hot.
Correct:	The delicate carrots so carefully and skilfully baked into this delicious pie *are* steaming hot.

The subject of the sentence is not the pie, but rather the carrots. Of course the pie *is* hot, but the verb must agree with the subject, not with the nearest noun.

Simple prepositional phrases can also lead to problems, since a singular noun can be followed by a preposition tat takes a plural object, or a plural noun can be followed by a preposition that takes a singular object. Be careful to make the verb agree with the *subject*.

- The *box* full of Christmas decorations *is* ready. (The *box* is ready.)
- The *planes* on runway twelve *are taxiing* for takeoff. (The *planes are taxiing*.)

Note that certain nouns ending in *–s*, like *statistics, mathematics*, and *politics,* are singular, not plural. Also a book title that contains a plural, such as *The Furies*, names one book, and is singular.

C.   VERBAL PHRASES

Certain phrases based on verbs are not in themselves parts of speech, but they can appear in sentences as various parts of speech. The entire phrase contains the verb form and all the words connected with it.

i)   **Infinitives** contain *infinitives* (the root of the verb preceded by *to*) and can act as nouns.

- *To run* is healthy. (The infinitive is the subject.)
- I plan *to run*. (The infinitive is the direct object.)
- His plan is *to fly commercial jets*. (The infinitive phrase is the noun complement, or subjective complement.)

ii)   **Gerunds** contain nouns that are made by adding *–ing* to verbs.

- *Swimming* is a healthy exercise. (The gerund is the subject.)
- *Staring at the noonday sun* is foolish. (The gerund phrase is the subject.)

iii)   **Participles** (also called **participials**) contain the **present participle** or the **past participle** and are used as adjectives.

- The exhausted boy fell asleep.
- The modern working woman is kept busy.
- The boy, whistling cheerfully, tossed bales of hay from the trailer.
- The boy, exhausted from the long day, fell asleep with his head on the last bale.

Notice that the last two examples could be rewritten in different form without the participial.

- The boy who was whistling cheerfully tossed bales of hay from the trailer.

The phrase, while still acting as an adjective, is now a dependent clause.

D.   PREPOSITIONS

Prepositions connect a noun or pronoun to other words or phrases.

- <u>Throw</u> the rope *into* <u>the boat</u>.
- We'll be <u>ready</u> *by* <u>Monday</u>.
- We'll <u>meet</u> *after* <u>school</u>.
- You'd better <u>talk</u> *to* <u>him</u>.

A **prepositional phrase** is the entire group of words that contain the preposition:

- We'll continue to the end.

Like verbs, prepositions take objects. The object of a preposition is the noun or pronoun that is being linked to some other part of speech. (In the examples above, the objects are boat, Monday, school, him, end.)

Usage Notes

Prepositions cause problems with grammatical agreement because a singular pronoun can be followed by a preposition with a plural object. The verb agrees with the subject of the sentence, not with the object of the preposition:

- *Each* of the boys *was* disqualified. (*Each was*, not *boys were*.)
- *Twelve* of the boys *were* disqualified. (Now *disqualified* refers to a plural noun.)

This kind of error is common. Remember to proofread carefully for agreement of noun and verb whenever a singular noun is followed by a preposition that takes a plural object.

E.   PROUNOUNS

Pronouns take the place of nouns: I, she, it, we, that, all, whatever, some.

Usage Notes: Clear Antecedents

There must be no misunderstanding regarding the nouns to which your pronouns refer.

- Both girls agreed that their projects had been prepared thoroughly. They were ready for the science fair. (What or who was ready? The girls? The projects?)
- When I got to the tax office, they told me they were closing for the day. (This sentence is fine for informal speech, but in standard written English, they can only refer to the tax office. A tax office cannot be they.)

When writing, check your pronouns and check that their antecedents are clear.

Usage Notes: The Correct Case

For the most part, English is not inflected. That means that most words do not change their endings to show how they are used in sentences.[*] Pronouns are one exception: they are inflected. Pronouns have three cases as shown in the following chart.

Whenever you use these pronouns, be aware of **pronoun case** and check for the correct spelling.			
Subjective case used for the subject of a sentence or clause, and for the complement of a linking verb	**Objective case used for the object of a verb or preposition, gerund, participle, or infinitive**	**Possessive case used to show ownership**	
		Used as an adjective	**Used as a subject or as the complement of a linking verb**
I	me	my	mine
you	you	your	yours
he/she/it	him/her/it	his/her/its	his/hers/its
we	us	our	ours
you	you	your	yours
they	them	their	theirs
who	whom	whose	whose

The possessive pronoun *its* follows EXACTLY THE SAME PATTERN as *his, hers, yours, theirs*. The possessive of pronouns is NEVER formed with an apostrophe.

When the pronoun is the subject, use the **subjective case**.

- *You* have been elected.
- Despite the weather, *we* are certainly going.
- *He* and *she* ran the marathon.
- Even after a late start, *they* still won the marathon.

If the pronoun is the subject and a possessive, use the second form of the **possessive case**.

- *Mine* is nearly ready.
- *Yours* is already finished, but *theirs* is not ready.

---

[*] Some typical noun and adjective endings are listed in this guide. These endings are a holdover from the days when English was an inflected language. Now we simply regard the endings as part of the word.

When the pronoun is the object (direct or indirect), use the **objective case**.

- Give it to *her*.
- The government mailed *me* a letter.
- The fall smashed *it* to pieces.
- When the paper is ready, give *it* to *her* and *me*.

A pronoun following a linking verb is a noun complement (or predicate nominative, or subject completion) and it is in the **subjective case**.

- It is *he*.
- Yes, I've seen Miss Jones. It was *she* that walked past just now.
- I am *he*.
- It is *I*.

These examples suggest the problem of different levels of language in different situations. Consider the sentence, *It is I.* The sentence is correct—but it might appear to be stuffy, even pretentious. However, in a formal or solemn context, such sentences are not only correct, they are suitable. On the other hand, in everyday life, few would complain about, *It's me*.

Sometimes the pronoun agreements cause trouble. Here is a useful rule of thumb:

Most of those who might say *Him and me did it*, would never say *Me did it* or *Him did it*. Whenever you have more than one pronoun, try the sentence with one of the pronouns at a time.

He did it + *I* did it = *He* and *I* did it.

She is the one + *He* is the one = *She* and *he* are the ones.

When the pronoun after a linking verb is a possessive, use the form of the possessive case that would be used for the subject of a sentence.

- The red one is *mine*. Did you hear me? *Mine* is the red one.
- This car is *hers*—or is it *theirs*? No, *theirs* is the car on the right.

Note the difference when a pronoun is used as an adjective and when it is used as a predicate complement:

- *Their* win was amazing.
- The win was *theirs*.

You would not want to memorize all the pronouns, but it is a good idea to be aware of them and their uses.

Kinds of Pronouns	Examples
Demonstrative I want to enter *this* in the exhibition.	This, that, these, those
Interrogative *Who* said that?	Who, whom, which, what, whoever, whomever, whichever, whatever
Relative Choose *whichever* you like.	Who, whom, that, which, whoever, whomever, whichever
Indefinite *Many* have asked that question.	All, another, any, anybody, anyone, anything, each, everybody, everyone, everything, few, many, nobody, none, one, several, some, somebody, someone
Reflexive She did the job *herself*.	Myself, yourself, herself, himself, itself, ourselves, yourselves, themselves
Intensive The professor *himself* was not sure of the answer.	Myself, yourself, herself, himself, itself, ourselves, yourselves, themselves

Notice the **reflexive** and **intensive** pronouns. These are often used incorrectly—often by people who are uneasily aware that pronoun case can be tricky, and who use the reflexive as a compromise: *Give it to myself*. The examples in the chart above show the only correct uses of the reflexive pronoun. Notice that when the reflexive is used immediately after the noun, then it is an **intensifier**.

And what about the pronouns *who* and *whom*? Although the distinction between these two pronouns may be disappearing, you should be able to use both of them in formal writing.

Who is an interrogative **subjective pronoun**. Use it whenever the pronoun is the subject of a sentence or a clause.

- *Who* are you?
- *Who* is going?
- The candidate *who* should be elected is Jesse.

Whom is an **interrogative objective pronoun**. Use it whenever the pronoun is the object of a predicate or a preposition.

- The prize will be given to *whom*?
- *Whom* did you tell?
- To *whom* did they refer?

> A simple **mnemonic**[*] for remembering the difference is to think "he/who" and "him/whom."
> If the sentence could use *he*, then use *who*; if the sentence could use *him*, then use *whom*.

- *He* will win. *Who* will win?
- Give it to *him*. Give it to *whom*?
- The crowd followed after *him*. The crowd followed after *whom*?
- The robbers left *him* for dead. The robbers left *whom* for dead?
- For *him*, we would do anything. For *whom* would we do anything?
- Yes, it is *he* that won. *Who* was it that won?

Of course, there is an extra mental step if the pronoun is not masculine.

- Give it to *her*. Give it to *whom*?
- For *her*, we would do anything. For *whom* would we do anything?
- Yes, it is *she* that won. *Who* was it that won?

F.   ADJECTIVES

Adjectives modify nouns.

- **describing**: a *grey* day, a *long* walk, his *wearisome* argument
- **limiting**: *one* child, *that* book, *my* car

Adjectives can be **participle** or verbs acting as adjectives.

- a *smoking* volcano
- a rotted log

Adjectives can be **infinitives**, which are either verbs in infinitive form or verb phrases containing an infinitive.

- The job *to do* is this.
- The man *to do the job* is Arthur.
- His sudden decision *to confess* was a shock.

Adjectives can be prepositional phrases.

- That child *on the edge of the cliff* is in great danger.

Adjectives can be **subordinate clauses**.

- The boy *who won the Governor General's Medal* is now a trained firefighter.

Although an **appositive** is a noun or a noun substitute (a nominal), adjectives can also have appositives. These are examples of **appositive adjectives**:

- The old man, *lean and stooped*, waited patiently by the door.
- *Lean and stooped*, the old man waited patiently.

---

[*] A **mnemonic** is a mental technique for making remembering easier. In the example, the identical final consonant sounds (hi**m**/who**m**) is a help to remembering that the correct use of *whom* is similar to the correct use of *him*.

Some adjectives have distinctive endings that might be useful when considering new kinds of adjectives.

-able/-ible bearable, sensible

-al, artful, brutal

-ful useful, handful, fanciful

-ic frantic, choleric

-ive intrusive, massive

-less hopeless, friendless

-ous officious, generous

Remembering the example given under nouns, you could invent an adjective for a special effect, and you might say (in the case of too many telephone calls) that, *This telephonic barrage is driving me crazy.*

G.   **ADVERBS**

Adverbs modify

- **verbs** (running *slowly*; *quickly* jumped)
- **adjectives** (*furiously* angry; *completely* red)
- **adverbs** (*quite* quickly; *completely* freely)

Adverbs modify by showing

- how (adverbs of manner) *quietly, fiercely*
- where (adverbs of place) in the country, on the stove
- why (adverbs of reason) *to avoid injury*
- when (adverbs of time) *before school*
- how often (adverbs of degree) *often, every day*

The only adverbial ending that remains in English is *ly*. Although nearly every word ending in *ly* is an adverb, not all adverbs end the same way, and a few adjectives (*lovely, lonely, deadly, friendly, likely, lively*) have the *ly* ending.

Usage Notes

Adverbs are frequently a source of errors in grammatical agreement.

- *The car went real fast* is not standard English because adverbs, not adjectives, should be used to modify adjectives. Use *really*.
- *I feel badly* is incorrect because a linking verb should be followed by an adjective, not an adverb. Use *bad*.

Either nouns or adjectives can follow sentences that contain a linking verb.

- He is a *runner*.
- He is *quick*.

This rule only applies to linking verbs. Other verbs in similar sentences are followed by adverbs, not adjectives.

> **Incorrect**: He runs *quick*.

> **Correct**: He runs *quickly*.

In this case, the verb *runs* must be followed by an adverb, *quickly*.

> Adjectives are limited in their propositions. They are found immediately before, or immediately after, the nouns they modify, or else they are found after linking a verb. Adverbs can be found almost anywhere in a sentence.

And here is a last note on adverbs and adjectives:

Every day is an adverb.

- They exercise *every day*.

Everyday is an adjective.

- Our *everyday* price is clearly marked.

H. CONJUNCTIONS

Conjunctions connect sentences and sentence parts. **Coordinating** conjunctions join equal parts.

- cake *and* ice-cream
- She stopped *and* she turned *and* she smiled.

Subordinating conjunctions join unequal parts.

- *Whenever* I hear that song, I want to laugh.

The parts are unequal because the first part is a subordinate clause that cannot stand alone, while the second part is an independent clause and is a sentence in its own right.

Conjunctions include *and, but, when, because*, and *either-or*.

I. INTERJECTIONS

Interjections usually express emotions or add intensity

- *Ouch*, that hurts!
- *Ah*! Now it's clear.
- *Umm* . . . I'm not sure.
- *Yes*, you must do it.

3. SYNTAX OF THE SENTENCE

A. KINDS OF SENTENCES

- **Declarative** sentences make statements.
- **Interrogative** sentences ask questions.
- **Exclamatory** sentences express strong emotion.
- **Imperative** sentences give instructions or commands.

Remember that exclamation marks and exclamatory sentences should rarely be used except in dialogue.

B. SENTENCE STRUCTURES

How long would you be able to read sentences like these?

Alyana arrived home. It was four o'clock. She turned on the radio. She listened to the news. She cut up potatoes and carrots. She cut up onions. She made a vegetable casserole. She put the casserole in the oven. She started her homework.

You probably would not put up with this sort of thing for long. Now, what about these sentences?

When Alyana arrived home, it was four o'clock. She turned on the radio to listen to the news while she cut up potatoes, carrots and onions for a vegetable casserole. As soon as she had put the casserole in the oven, she started her homework.

The combining of sentences and the use of subordination have improved the simple primer* style of the first paragraph.

i) Simple

An independent clause (a sentence) containing one subject and one verb makes a simple sentence.

- *The boy stood on the garden wall.*

Sentence order can be altered for variety or to emphasize one part of the sentence. The part to be emphasized usually comes first.

- *On the garden wall stood the boy.*

ii) Compound

Two independent clauses (or sentences) joined by a coordinating conjunction make a compound sentence.

- *The boy stood on the garden wall,* but *no one noticed him.*

With a small alteration, the sentence order can be changed.

- *No one noticed the boy* as *he stood on the garden wall.*

---

* Primer style is the very simple style found in the beginning readers for very young children.

iii) **Complex**

Two clauses joined by a subordinating conjunction make a complex sentence. One clause must be independent and one clause must be dependent (subordinate).

- *Although the boy stood on the garden wall*, no one noticed him.
- No one noticed the boy, *although he stood on the garden wall.*
- *While the firefighters were distracted by brush fires*, three houses burned to the ground.
- Three houses burned to the ground *while the firefighters were distracted by brush fires*.
- An actress *who has won three Oscars* will be present tonight.

Although the last example could be written in a different order, it might be better not to do so.

- Present tonight will be an actress *who has won three Oscars.*

iv) **Compound-Complex**

A compound-complex sentence contains at least **two independent clauses** and **one dependent clause**.

- *While I slept,* the sun rose and the birds began to sing.
- *Although she didn't win a medal,* Janine competed at the Olympics and she has never forgotten the wonderful experience.

When writing or editing, be aware of your sentences and their structure. Consider varying sentence structure, length, and order both for variety and for emphasis. Use transitional devices (words like *although, next, consequently*) to order and link ideas.

ORDERING INFORMATION

All School Orders

School Authorities are eligible to purchase these resources by applying the Learning Resource Credit Allocation (LRCA – 25% school discount) on their purchase through the Learning Resources Centre (LRC). Call LRC for details.

THE KEY *Study Guides* are specifically designed to assist students in preparing for unit tests, final exams, and provincial examinations.

KEY Study Guides – $29.95 each plus G.S.T.

SENIOR HIGH		JUNIOR HIGH	ELEMENTARY
Biology 30 Chemistry 30 English 30-1 English 30-2 Math 30 (Pure) Math 30 (Applied) Physics 30 Social Studies 30 Social Studies 33	Biology 20 Chemistry 20 English 20-1 Math 20 (Pure) Physics 20 Social Studies 20 English 10-1 Math 10 (Pure) Science 10 Social Studies 10	Language Arts 9 Math 9 Science 9 Social Studies 9 Math 8 Math 7	Language Arts 6 Math 6 Science 6 Social Studies 6 Math 4 Language Arts 3 Math 3

Student Notes and Problems (SNAP) Workbooks contain complete explanations of curriculum concepts, examples, and exercise questions.

SNAP Workbooks – $29.95 each plus G.S.T.

SENIOR HIGH		JUNIOR HIGH	ELEMENTARY
Chemistry 30 Math 30 Pure Math 30 Applied Math 31 Physics 30	Chemistry 20 Math 20 Pure Math 20 Applied Physics 20 Math 10 Pure Math 10 Applied Science 10	Math 9 Science 9 Math 8 Math 7	Math 6 Math 5 Math 4 Math 3

Visit our website for a "tour" of resource content and features at
www.castlerockresearch.com

#2340, 10180 – 101 Street
Edmonton, AB Canada T5J 3S4
e-mail: learn@castlerockresearch.com

Phone: 780.448.9619
Toll-free: 1.800.840.6224
Fax: 780.426.3917

2006 (3)

SCHOOL ORDER FORM

Castle Rock Research Corp

THE KEY

THE KEY	QUANTITY
Biology 30	
Chemistry 30	
English 30-1	
English 30-2	
Math30 (Pure)	
Math 30 (Applied)	
Physics 30	
Social Studies 30	
Social Studies 33	
Biology 20	
Chemistry 20	
English 20-1	
Math 20 (Pure)	
Physics 20	
Social Studies 20	
English 10-1	
Math 10 (Pure)	
Science 10	
Social Studies 10	
Language Arts 9	
Math 9	
Science 9	
Social Studies 9	
Math 8	
Math 7	
Language Arts 6	
Math 6	
Science 6	
Social Studies 6	
Math 4	
Math 3	
Language Arts 3	

SNAP WORKBOOKS
Notes and Problems/ Student Notes and Problems

SNAP WORKBOOKS	QUANTITY	
	Workbooks	Solutions Manuals
Chemistry 30		
Chemistry 20		
Physics 30		
Physics 20		
Math 30 Pure		
Math 30 Applied		
Math 31		
Math 20 Pure		
Math 20 Applied		
Math 10 Pure		
Math 10 Applied		
Science 10		
Science 9		
Math 9		
Math 8		
Math 7		
Math 6		
Math 5		
Math 4		
Math 3		

TOTALS

KEYS

WORKBOOKS

SOLUTION MANUALS

Learning Resources Centre

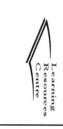

Castle Rock Research is pleased to announce an exclusive distribution arrangement with the Learning Resources Centre (LRC). Under this agreement, schools can now place all their orders with LRC for order fulfillment. As well, these resources are eligible for applying the Learning Resource Credit Allocation (LRCA), which gives schools a 25% discount off LRC's selling price. Call LRC for details.

Orders may be placed with LRC by
telephone: (780) 427-5775
fax: (780) 422-9750
internet: **www.lrc.learning.gov.ab.ca**
or mail: **12360 - 142 Street NW
Edmonton, AB T5L 4X9**

PAYMENT AND SHIPPING INFORMATION

Name: _____

School Telephone: _____

SHIP TO
School: _____
Address: _____
City: _____ Postal Code: _____

PAYMENT
☐ by credit card
VISA/MC Number: _____ Expiry Date: _____
Name on Card: _____
☐ enclosed cheque
☐ invoice school   P.O. number: _____

#2340, 10180 – 101 Street, Edmonton, AB T5J 3S4
email: learn@castlerockresearch.com
Tel: 780.448.9619   Fax: 780.426.3917
Toll-free: 1.800.840.6224
www.castlerockresearch.com
2006 (4)